GARDEN DESIGN

■ Planning Smaller Gardens ■

Brian Leverett

CROWOOD GARDENING GUIDES

First published in 1989 by
The Crowood Press
Ramsbury, Marlborough
Wiltshire SN8 2HE

British Library Cataloguing in Publication Data
Leverett, Brian
  Garden design: planning smaller gardens
  1. Gardens. Landscape design. Amateurs' manuals
  I. Title
  712'.6

ISBN 1-85223-149-1

Line illustrations by Claire Upsdale-Jones

Picture Credits

Geoff Moore of Dorset Media Services for the Frontispiece and Figs 2, 12, 46, 48, 57, 58, 59, 78, and 85; Derek Gould for Figs 4, 15, 17, 27, 41, 51, 52, 53, 54, 56, 70, and 82; Bruce Grant-Braham for Figs 3, 67, 80, 81, 87, 88, 89, and 90; Commander David Aldrich for Figs 10 and 11; Mrs Sue Willows for Figs 25, 32, 33, 66, 68, 74, 75, 79, 83, 84, and 91; Michael and Lois Warren (Photos Horticultural) for Figs 6, 26, 34, 36, 38, and 45; Michael Boys for Fig 31; and Bob and Liz Gibbons (Natural Image) for Figs 1, 19, 21, 77, and 86.

Michael Warren for the front cover; Geoff Moore of Dorset Media Services for the back cover (top); and Mrs Sue Willows for the back cover (bottom).

Typeset by Avonset, Midsomer Norton, Bath
Printed in Spain by Graficromo s.a., Cordoba

Contents

Introduction

The development of the garden runs in parallel with the architecture that it complements. The first gardens built in the British Isles date from the time of the Romans, who imported Mediterranean ideas and culture to any lands that they conquered. As well as a knowledge of garden building and design they brought with them plants from their homelands – new vegetables, flowers to brighten the dull islands, and, above all, the herbs that were necessary for their cookery, especially sage, rosemary, thyme and coriander. They also brought trees to provide timber and nuts, particularly walnuts and flowering shrubs, all of which escaped from the gardens and rapidly naturalised, so that today few of us can distinguish the immigrant from what seems to be the true native.

With the retreat of the Romans, gardens, along with so much of the newly-established culture, disappeared, and Britain reverted to its previous savage state. It was not until the feudal system started to break down in the fourteenth century (following the Black Death), that the population began farming small areas of land, rented from the lord of the manor. Previously, they had been in the position of serfs working for their lord. Horticulture became more important – for example, medicine at this time depended almost entirely upon herbs, as did the cookery of the period. Herbs were essential to conceal the taste of the dull, monotonous foods, and began to be cultivated outside homes.

The Renaissance in Italy saw a change in the common style of warfare – the castle no longer afforded total protection, and therefore a new type of architecture was developed, and buildings came to be artistic as well as functional.

With this development began gardening as we know it today, and an outstanding feature of these early times was the maze at Hampton Court. Large Elizabethan manor houses were built in the shape of the letter 'E', adorned with knot gardens with neat, trimmed hedges enclosing not only herbs, but also flowers. These were still mainly native and naturalised together with any sports or mutations, such as double forms of common flowers, like soapwort, which were subsequently cultivated both for their beauty and their novelty value.

The great fortunes that were made out of trade in the seventeenth and eighteenth centuries led to an increase in the building of large houses with laid-out parks, and landscape gardening 'came of age' overnight. The gardens of the rich and poor were to develop in vastly different ways. The wealthy had gardens for pleasure, gardens to delight the eye, gardens to provide them with a rich variety of fruit and vegetables throughout the year. A new invention – the greenhouse or conservatory – was heated in order to recreate a tropical climate, and exotic fruits such as oranges and pineapples could be cultivated and enjoyed. When the rich moved to London in the winter (as the social season demanded), their gardeners in the country would send them fresh fruit and vegetables daily. Exotic subjects such as orchids became commonplace in the houses of the aristocracy. To satisfy this growing interest in gardening, plant hunters left Europe to seek out new varieties, returning with dahlias and fuchsias from the Americas, new shrubs and flowers from the Himalayas and, from the mysterious east, roses that would bloom all the year round. All these were imported, together with a range of other wondrous plants. The garden had a new role – it had become a status symbol, a position it has retained to the present day. In addition to the gardens themselves, parklands were created in the grounds of the houses of the aristocracy. Landscaping took over from the plants themselves, and became, in the eyes of the very rich, the ultimate symbol of wealth, as important to the culture of post-Elizabethan Britain as architecture or the arts.

Whilst the rich saw plants as a luxury, the poor who lived in the country used gardening in a different way. By today's standards, many of them had very large gardens (as can be seen from remaining farm labourers' cottages) – these were purely functional, and very much a part of the rural economy. They would grow most of the food that they required – mainly potatoes and turnips – and also raise a few pigs to provide them with bacon. Around the door the wife would plant her herbs and decorative wild flowers, as well as putting in plants and cuttings acquired from the big house. Here lie the true origins of the 'cottage garden.' Plants were spread by this method of exchange, since there was certainly no spare money to spend on flowers at this stage.

Meanwhile, in the cities houses were built close together, usually without gardens. Where they were allowed for, they were invariably small plots which seldom flourished – the soil would become sour as a result of atmospheric pollution. The advent of clean air legislation in the 1950s has meant that the atmosphere is no longer polluted with sulphur, and now town gardens can be made to prosper in a way that was once thought to be the preserve of the countryside.

The modern garden is a phenomenon of the 1970s and 1980s, the product of a generation whose parents carried on with the 'Dig For Victory' campaign for many years after its official end. It was during the 1970s that garden centres emerged to cater for the requirements of the new leisure gardeners – these were ordinary people who tended the soil for pleasure and not as a means of survival.

This book is written to explain the various styles of gardening that are appropriate to today's modern smaller gardens, so that you may assess the approaches that are possible for your plot. It gives help on how to plan your plot, provides the basic practical details you will need to execute your plan, and gives some basic information on the requirements of plants, so that you may avoid the failures that the uninformed often suffer.

CHAPTER 1

The Plot

The development of the suburbs from the mid-nineteenth century onwards was to lead to gardens for all. These were invariably split into back gardens, in which vegetables and fruit were grown, and a front garden, which almost always consisted of a grass square or oblong around which flowers were planted. In this way, the garden reflected exactly the philosophy of the house itself – a back room for the family to live in and a front room reserved for visitors. This approach was to remain the norm until well after the Second World War. Today we no longer need to produce the majority of our own fruit and vegetables (although there is a strong case for growing some items, especially those that are difficult to obtain fresh in the shops). However, there are now new pressures on the land, especially in those parts of the country where work is situated or where there are special leisure facilities. We find that the majority of houses occupy less than a tenth of an acre where once they would have enjoyed curtilages of twice this size. The smaller gardens that have resulted from modern building policies require more careful landscaping than their predecessors. They demand 'micro-landscaping', where every square metre is made to realise its fullest potential and where the worth of every plant grown should be appreciated to the full.

THE CASE FOR LANDSCAPING

It is only when a garden is positively designed that it is possible to derive the maximum benefit from it. With a little foresight the well-designed garden may be achieved without any more effort (and possibly less) than needs to be expended upon the 'accidental' garden, which comes together as the result of unplanned, haphazard plantings. For many years there was only one style of garden thought suitable for the suburbs – a square or rectangular lawn surrounded by a border of haphazardly-placed plants. It was certainly not considered necessary to landscape small plots. This approach to design in the garden is now as archaic as the wallpaper, border, picture-rail style of interior decoration that was in vogue at the same time. Unfortunately, ideas on how subjects should be treated outside the house tend to change much more slowly than those concerned with the inside. Nevertheless, attention is beginning to move away from the house in terms of design – many houses have their own designer-produced kitchens and bedrooms, and the same thought and effort is now being put into developing the area outside the house. The garden is the house's natural extension, its exterior decoration. Just as central heating and double glazing increase the value of a property, a well-landscaped garden greatly adds to its worth. Houses which are all built to the same design, and situated in the same street, may have widely differing values because of secondary features such as the state of decoration. It is impossible to quantify these items, since their effect on would-be purchasers is rather subjective, but the state of the garden will often lead to initial interest, and it will usually continue to influence throughout an inspection of the premises. Even if the garden does not directly raise the value of a property, it is extremely unlikely that you will achieve the best possible price unless it is well laid-out and tidy.

Fig 1 A small town garden where the design reflects its use as an extension of the house.

People seldom remain in a house for longer than ten years these days, and financial considerations will therefore be of as much importance as aesthetics to some people. Moreover, virtually all of the work can be done by the average person – no special skills are required (although being physically fit helps!). This means that the potential for increasing the value of the property per pound spent is far greater than with those tasks which have to be performed by paid labour.

It is possible to have a garden designed and landscaped by a professional, and some are very good, offering an excellent service and value. It can, however, be extremely difficult to distinguish these from the 'cowboys' and crooks, and even the honest jobber may lack the imagination that you yourself can bring to your plot. To him it is just another source of income, while to you it is a home! The profit margins of some professional can be omitted from your plans entirely!

PLANNING

The strongest urge once you have acquired a garden is to rush out to the plot, spade in hand, and start clearing the ground. Resist the temptation! Before you consider doing any physical work it is important to draw up a detailed plan. Not only can this avoid unnecessary physical work, but you may also discover features in the garden that it is desirable to retain.

It is advisable to consider all aspects of the law as far as it affects gardens, but there are two important features that must be looked into before any work is undertaken. Tree preservation orders exist to protect those trees whose importance extends beyond the boundaries of an individual property, and if trees are covered by an order and you fell them you may be liable for a substantial fine for each one. The protection

Fig 2 *The house and gardens are not separate entities, but should blend together to form the whole.*

is not limited to felling, and you have to obtain the permission of the planning authority if you wish to prune or crown lift the tree. Any tree (other than a fruit tree), may be made the subject of a tree preservation order, so before any work is undertaken upon trees, check with your local town planning authority that there is no restriction. It is best to be sure. If there is, then you will have to apply for permission to carry out the necessary work. Even where there are no legal impediments to felling trees, you should still give careful consideration before applying the axe – trees take several years to reach maturity, and once they have been removed it will probably take you a lifetime to replace them.

When you are planning a new garden, see if there are any features of the old garden that you wish to retain. Consider whether a scheme could be adapted to incorporate them – age, whether

in the form of a tree or well-weathered rock, adds an extra dimension, and is essential to the illusion of peace and tranquillity that most people seek from their garden. With ingenuity it is possible to adapt that which is immovable – for example, old tree trunks may function as supports for climbing subjects. Alternatively, if they are cut close to the ground, the centre can be scooped out, filled with loam and then planted with low-growing rock plants. The wood of the tree will function in a similar manner to the stones of the rockery. Nothing in your garden need ever be an eyesore.

The other legal factor to be considered concerns open-plan gardens. Covenants may exist which restrict the building of hedges and fences, and these will need to be checked in the deeds of the house. Again, if there is any doubt, contact the town planning office. They may have originally enforced the restriction, but some authorities are becoming more reasonable in their interpretation of open-plan schemes, having become aware of the problems that dogs can create in such estates. The laws relating to planning permissions are somewhat complex. In many instances you do not require permission to erect a greenhouse, but there are exceptions. To avoid any expensive misunderstandings, contact your local planning department for advice on what you may or may not erect without permission – this advice is free to any interested party.

Having established your legal position, you need to decide exactly the role of the garden and the amount of time that you are prepared to spend upon its maintenance. Unless you have planned your garden well, you can easily become a slave to it, and it may take all of your free time during the summer months, leaving you no opportunity to enjoy it. Some people will wish their garden to occupy much of their time, and will almost be seeking a second career from it, especially if they are retired, but such an approach will not work in a household where both partners go out to work or where there are small children. Remember, too, that young families will make special demands upon a site, with the necessity to provide a reasonably-sized grass playing area, and to leave large trees which can become homes and hidden areas which can turn into secret gardens. These, much more than material wealth, are the real joys of childhood.

Watering is another factor to be considered at a very early stage. Bedding plants and the immaculate lawns that are such important features of the formal-type garden will require almost constant watering during a dry spell if they are to prosper. It is pointless adopting this style of gardening if you intend to spend a large part of the summer away from home on vacation or business, unless you can make alternative arrangements with a neighbour to ensure that watering is regular. Where this is not possible, you may be restricted to a herbaceous or mixed bed.

THE SOIL

The secret of successful horticulture is to be at peace with your garden. Individual plants have different requirements. Some plants require direct sunlight, others shade; some need damp conditions whilst others require a well-drained soil. Many plants, such as the birch, are tolerant of a range of chemical conditions, whilst others are sensitive to the least change in the chemical environment (such as those alpines whose leaves turn yellow as a result of a small amount of alkali being leached out of the limestone of a rockery). It is not in the least necessary to possess a deep knowledge of science to garden successfully, and many people who lack a formal education have mastered the art of horticulture. Invariably, they received their skills passed down by word of mouth from the previous generation – father to son and mother to daughter. In today's competitive world it is a sad fact that parents no longer attach importance to passing on gardening skills, even where they possess them. Moreover, whereas former generations tended to settle in the area in which they were brought up, where they would be familiar with the soil and climate, the greater mobility of labour has meant that today's young householders may find themselves in an environment far removed from that of their youth. However, anyone can achieve a reasonable degree of success, even without any previous experience of the subject, as long as he understands some of the fundamental principles which govern gardening.

Acids, Alkalis and pH

There are several different types of acids and alkalis and they differ very much in their action. For example, acetic and sulphuric are both acids, but, while sulphuric acid is so strong that it will burn the skin, acetic acid can be taken into the body (usually in the form of vinegar). As the strength of both acids and alkalis can also vary, scientists have come up with a scale that simultaneously compares both the amount and the strength of the acids and alkalis present – the pH scale. Water (the universal neutral substance) is given the value 7, and anything with a value below this is an acid, while those substances with the value above it are alkalis. The full range is from 0 to 14, but you will rarely encounter conditions far removed from the central values. The range in which plants grow well is very limited – from about 5.5 to 8.5 – but it must be remembered that a decrease of 1.0 pH unit corresponds to a tenfold increase in acidity, and an increase of 1.0 pH unit represents a tenfold increase in alkalinity (or reduction in acidity).

The pH of any soil may be tested using an acid testing kit, obtainable from most garden centres. This consists of a collection of dyes, blended to give a super dye which is very sensitive to changes in pH. The dye is added to a sample of water with which the soil has been shaken, and it produces a colour which is then compared with a standard colour chart provided. In this way, the acidity or alkalinity is indicated. The accuracy of the test will depend upon the care with which the sample of soil was collected. It is possible to obtain completely wrong results for the garden as a whole if just one sample is taken from one area – the conditions in that area may not be typical of the garden in general. You should, therefore, take samples at evenly distributed distances throughout the whole area of the garden, at a depth of 2–6in (5–15cm), and mix all of the soil together thoroughly. Allow the soil to fall into a heap, split the heap into four and take the two diagonally opposing quarters, discarding the remainder. Thoroughly mix the portion that you have retained and again reduce its volume to a half using the same method. Continue the process until you have a sample of the size required to perform the test. In this way you will have a truly representative sample that will give you an accurate result for your garden as a whole.

Soil may also be tested to establish the level of certain elements, particularly potassium (potash) and phosphorus (phosphate). This is generally not necessary, and need not be attempted as a routine test before planning the garden. You will, however, have to employ such tests should the plants fail to grow or if they are seen to suffer from severe stunted growth.

The most important factors in any garden are the *aspect* and the *soil* itself. There are several different types of soil, although they do approximate to four main types.

Loamy Soil

Loamy soil is the best of all soils for any type of garden, consisting of small grains of sand (silica) together with a large quantity of decaying humus (vegetable or animal matter). Ideal loam would come from a meadow which has been in cultivation for many years, and in a garden its depth should preferably be in excess of 18in (45cm). Such soil is often only associated with older properties, but if a building development has taken place on farmland it is possible to encounter this type of soil even on a new housing estate. Loam is the type of soil that you will need to obtain if you are going to buy topsoil, or if you are compounding a mixture for filling containers or as a base for a rockery.

Small quantities of loam can be made continually in the garden for compounding sowing and seed composts. Cut turves to a depth of 2in (5cm) and then stack them one on top of another, with the grass side face downwards so that it is touching the soil of the turf beneath. Allow the soil to remain until it is a homogeneous, friable mass.

Light Sandy Soils

Lighter, sandy soils lack the body provided by the moisture- and nutrient-retaining humus, and consequently they tend to dry out very quickly and become impoverished. The result of this is that many plants will not prosper on them and those plants that do grow are frequently stunted. In addition, they tend to be very cold soils – their light colour reflects the sun's heat, whereas the dark, humus-laden soils absorb and retain much of the sun's energy. Sandy soils are often acidic and are ideal for heathers, rhododendrons and camellias, but even where these are grown it is best to include as much humus as is practical to aid the moisture, nutrient and heat retention. This can be done either by including peat, which in the quantities required could prove extremely expensive, or the composted leaves of deciduous trees. Large quantities of these can be gathered in the autumn free of charge and composted by storing for a year in a compost maker, or even on a simple heap, which can be turned every three months. After a year you will have good quality humus. (Note: You should never attempt to compost the leaves of conifers such as pine needles as these contain toxins which can adversely affect soil fertility.)

It is unlikely that you will be able to provide sufficient humus material in one treatment; the provision of this material should be considered as an ongoing operation. One method of providing humus material is to mulch each year, with deciduous leaves or even lawn mowings. This not only facilitates the retention of moisture during the current season, but the humus will also gradually be worked into the soil, aided by the action of the worm population which it will help to build up. It is far better to compost the dead plant material before adding to the soil if this is practical. One of the problems with light soils is that they are deficient in nutrients. Simply adding artificial fertilisers will not solve the problem. Water-soluble chemicals will dissolve in the rainfall and, there being very little humus material, the nutrient-rich water will pass into the water table, and the minerals will be leached from the soil.

Heavy Clay Soils

Heavy clay soils are made up of minute particles of mineral material cemented together, and are often rich in plant nutrients. However, they have the disadvantage that the nutrients tend to be locked in and they need to be released with lime. This presents no problems at all for the vegetable grower, but the landscape gardener will probably wish to work with some subjects that are not lime-tolerant. The most practical way to deal with clay soils is to add extra humus materials (as described for sandy soils). This has the advantage of opening up the soil. Clay soils are also very heavy to work, and it may be quite late in the spring before it is possible to get on to them to do any digging. It is advisable with all soils to complete the heavy digging in October before the worst of the weather sets in, and this is even more important with clay soils – not only are they far easier to work before they have become waterlogged, but the crystals of ice formed by the frost will tend to break up the soil into a fine tilth.

Chalk Soils

These are downland soils, with only a covering of loam, which yield good cereal and vegetable crops. Flowers and shrubs can also be grown successfully on them, but you will need to be aware of flowers which are not tolerant of chalk. Chalk soils tend to be well drained, but initial digging is extremely hard work.

FERTILISERS

The plant will provide for itself the vast majority of its nutritional requirements by means of photosynthesis. In addition, it will require nitrogen to produce the large amount of proteins that it needs; phosphorus, which as phosphates combines with protein to form important substances (enzymes) in the plant; and potash or potassium which is required for flower formation. Certain trace elements, that is, other minerals required in only minute amounts, are also necessary. The best way of providing these is by means of decaying animal products, manure, fish meal, blood or spent mushroom compost. An extra boost may be given by means of artificial fertilisers such as the balanced 'Growmore', sulphate of ammonia (provides nitrogen), sulphate of potash (provides potassium), or phosphate of ammonia (provides nitrogen and phosphate simultaneously). Artificial fertilisers have an advantage over manures because they are in a form that plants can utilise immediately. Only small quantities should be applied for specific purposes (for example a potash fertiliser around narcissi bulbs during the flowering and dying-down period – this will ensure that they retain their ability to flower in future years, otherwise they may go blind). Great care must be taken to ensure that the crystals do not come into contact with the plants as the chemicals may burn them. Artificial fertilisers should not be thought of as an alternative to manuring – they are extremely soluble and are soon lost from the soil, which they do nothing to improve in the long term. You should be seeking to improve the quality of the soil continually, otherwise it will revert to its former impoverished state. Unless you have access to a supply of farmyard manure (which should not be applied until it is well rotted), you should make the only worthwhile substitute – compost.

COMPOST MAKING

The secret of good compost making is to ensure a steady supply. Dig a pit 10in (25cm) deep, 3ft (1m) wide by 9ft (3m) long. Collect all forms of plant material (except pine needles) and break up as small as is practical. Stack the material in the pit to a height of 6in (15cm). Mix up the different types of vegetable matter – any weed seeds or perennial roots will be destroyed by the composting process. Cover with 1in (2.5cm) of loam and then add a compost activator (obtainable from any garden centre). Compost is formed by the process of fermentation, in which micro-organisms present in the loam gradually break down the plant material. These microbes of decay need moisture which they can usually obtain from the plant matter itself. Cover with plastic sheeting to ensure that the eco-system

Fig 3 Primroses will flourish in shady spots, providing they have a rich soil and moist conditions. Having flowered they retreat for the rest of the year when there are other subjects of interest in the garden.

does not flood during a storm – this would stop the compost making process. It is not necessary to aerate the heap.

As you move across the pit gradually stacking more and more material, the first greenery will, in a matter of months, have been converted into compost. It will be ready for use when it is homogenous – when it is no longer possible to distinguish between the individual pieces of plant material from which it was made. Compost can be made in a vertical compost maker. This consists of a framework into which movable boards may be fitted – pieces of wooden pallets are ideal for the purpose. A layer of plant material is built up to 6in (15cm) over the whole floor, and this is covered with 2in (5cm) of loam, followed by a sprinkling of compost activator. The process is then repeated continually until the top of the container (which can be of any height) is reached. The bottom boards are removed and the friable compost is shovelled out when it is ready.

Every type of soil will be improved by the addition of humus material and will grow virtually any type of plant, including the acid-lovers – but, again, it is advisable to live in peace with your garden and, if in doubt, omit the acid-loving plants. It is fairly easy to supply the correct condition for the smaller rooted plants – simply dig out an area to the depth that the roots will penetrate, and fill in the hole formed with composted leaves or peat before planting. It is almost impossible to achieve the correct conditions for the deep tap-rooted specimens and totally unachievable for most trees – both these require an extremely large space for their roots. Few gardens will have a constant depth of soil, and prized acid-lovers, such as camellias, can be planted where the greatest depth of soil exists above the chalk, if necessary. Rhododendrons may be grown successfully in about 12–18in (30–45cm) of acid soil, even on a chalky base, providing that they are mulched regularly with compost, as the roots do not penetrate to a great depth.

TOWN SOILS

Gardens associated with old town houses, or with new houses built upon old sites, often have sour soils. This is the result of prolonged assault by acid rains, and years of industrial and other forms of air pollution. For years these gardens have grown very little, other than bulbs which have their own food store and which will flower when cultivated in the absence of any medium other than water. Even these obliging plants have to be replaced every year if worthwhile results are to be obtained. Such spoilt soils may be improved by the addition of lime which will neutralise the acid, and unlock the nutrients that the land contains. Initial application should be at the rate of 2oz/sq yd (60g/sq m). The soil should be dug over and re-tested to ascertain the new pH value, taking care to ensure that you have a truly representative sample, as a quantity of unmixed lime could give you an artificially high result. Treatment should be continued until a pH of from 5.5 to 6.0 is obtained, but really at best,

this approach is somewhat 'hit and miss' and extremely laborious. Most town gardens are small, so, if they do not support plant growth, the most suitable treatment is to remove the topsoil to a depth of about 24in (60cm) and replace it with good quality loam. The other approach is to build a patio and grow all your plants in containers. Container gardens are ideally suited to towns, but it is important to ensure that the brick and paving work is of the highest quality, and that brightly-coloured flowers are used to contrast with the subdued shades of the concrete.

THE CLIMATE

The British people never cease to complain about the climate, but it is the finest in the world for growing the greatest variety of plants. At least one member of every single family of plants can be grown in British gardens, and few other countries (if any) have the climate to create gardens of the same richness of variety. Nevertheless, the success with which various species grow in any individual garden will depend upon the local climate, and this may vary quite considerably from that of the country as a whole. The most important factor is the latitude – the further south, the earlier the flowering or cropping season for any species. The season in the south of Britain is at least a fortnight earlier than that in the north and, because of the colder conditions, the onset of winter and the autumnal frost is a fortnight or so earlier in the north than in the south. However, the effects of the Gulf Stream can have an even more pronounced effect than the latitude, and the warm waters bathing the south-west coast yield a climate that is far milder than would be anticipated from its geographical position alone. This area also receives an above-average rainfall. All this tends to make for sub-tropical conditions and, providing the minimum amount of winter protection is provided, it is possible to grow subjects such as palms in the open in coastal

Fig 4 Conifers will grow well under most conditions and make an excellent year-round garden which needs little maintenance.

towns. Such plants are usually only used by the municipal authorities, because of their size and the expense and expertise involved.

So, growth is far lusher in the gardens of the south-west as compared with the rest of the country. The position and aspect of any one garden, however, will create its own micro-climate which may either magnify or diminish the factors which together produce the local climate. In a particular garden there will be exposed positions, sheltered positions, positions in the shade, or on a south-facing wall which will receive extra sunlight. All of these factors will contribute to produce a variety of different micro-climates and growing conditions in different parts of the garden. In order to make the garden fulfil its potential, it is necessary to appreciate the various climatic factors from the outset, and these must be taken into account when designing the garden.

Sunshine

The amount of sunshine falling upon any part of the garden will depend upon its aspect – that is, its position in relation to the points of the compass. The first fact that must be appreciated by anyone seeking to design a garden is that every plot has a north-, east-, south- and west-facing aspect, and that each cardinal point should be considered as a separate entity within the overall plan. Should the four sides of the garden not correspond exactly to the points of the compass, treat each side as though it were in the position of the nearest point. The south-facing side, the most exposed part of which is at the north of the garden, will receive extra warmth and light. A brick wall facing south will absorb the radiant heat during the daytime and, when the ambient temperature drops, it will release this extra warmth, acting as a natural storage heater.

These factors mean that the position will be favourable to more delicate subjects, that otherwise would not prosper, and are often not thought of as plants that can be grown in Britain as well as in their natural tropical home. Do not be frightened to tackle the more exotic subjects, such as nectarines, which will provide flowers in the spring (autumnal gold in the autumn), together with fruits of a quality that no greengrocer can match with his imports. Conversely, the northern side will receive far less of the sun's warmth and, more importantly, light (a far more significant factor in the plant's growth). This means that only shade-loving plants, of which there are a great many, should be grown on this part of the plot. Light-coloured sandy soils will be much colder than dark soils that are rich in humus – the former will reflect much of the radiant heat from the sun, and will be less able to retain the heat that it receives. Consequently, they are more susceptible to frosts and the growing season is correspondingly reduced.

Wind

The wind is the enemy of the grower, causing wind burn, which is responsible for the death of many plants, especially young seedlings and cuttings, and the destruction of the leaves of even the most well-established subjects. The prevailing wind blows from the west to the east, and the western boundary should, therefore, function as a wind break. Solid structures will deflect the wind as in Fig 5(a), and it will be seen that immediately to the windward is a sheltered position as there is in the area immediately to the leeward. Providing that the plants do not exceed about 3ft (1m), those on the immediate leeward will most certainly prosper, and this is another small area that can be used for growing delicate subjects. However, it should not be considered as an alternative to the south-facing wall. It is not an ideal position, although it may be used for growing cordon and espalier fruit bushes, depending upon the amount of sunshine that it receives. On the windward side the wall will tend to shelter the plants from the sun until late in the day, whilst they will not suffer the wind burn of subjects 3ft (1m) or more in front of the wall. It is necessary to select partial shade-loving plants.

Far preferable to solid walls or fences are those with gaps. These are not always practical, but hedges which contain many spaces are an acceptable alternative. Rather than jump the hedge, some of the wind will pass through the gaps, whilst that which meets a solid obstacle will rise above it. The result of this is that the force of the wind is dissipated in all directions and is no longer as strong at any one position. Solid structures do not stop wind, but simply redirect it, deflecting it to a region of lesser constraint.

During the spring the wind tends to come from the north-east, resulting in damage to plants exposed to this aspect. Where there is an exposed northern aspect, only the hardiest subjects should be considered suitable. Draughts resulting from air currents being forced through the gap between two buildings sited closely together can result in the worst problems associated with wind damage. If such areas are to be used, and they receive sufficient wind to cause a tunnel effect, then a structure such as a fence must be constructed to function as a wind break, before anything can be grown successfully there. It may be the case that a very small area is receiving wind from an extremely large area (see Fig 5(b)).

The strength of the wind, the amount of rainfall, the temperature – and with it the likelihood of early and late frosts that can cause so many problems with half-hardy annuals – will depend upon the exact location of the garden. On the side of a hill the wind will be at its fiercest, with it gaining momentum to rise over the hill in the same way that it clears the wall. The effect will be less severe on the flat, while air currents will tend to skim across the top of valleys. Consequently, it is often possible to ignore the worst effects of wind at low levels, whereas when the house is situated on the side of a steep hill the effects must be taken into consideration. The exact location of a house is something that a

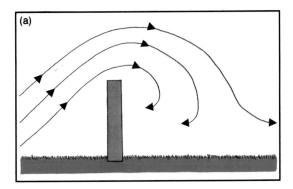

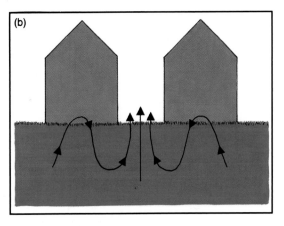

Fig 5 The dispersal of wind by obstacles.
(a) Wind clearing a wind break. There are two areas of comparatively still air – immediately before the wind break and immediately after. Providing the areas receive sufficient sunlight, either may be used to advantage.

(b) Winds from a large area concentrated through a gap, creating a draught. The area between two houses or other substantial buildings will tend to focus all the wind falling on to the structures, and unless a wind break is concentrated, this will be a hostile area for plant growth.

potential buyer might care to keep in mind if he is a keen gardener. He should realise from the outset that, with certain situations, the plants that grow happily outside five miles away, might not survive in his garden. If your site is exposed, on the side of the hill, you must take care to ensure that the glazing is regularly maintained – glass is frequently lost in such situations. Failure to check the glass one autumn can mean reglazing becoming essential the following spring. However, high ground is not necessarily bad – it may be quite the reverse, depending upon how exposed the site is. Where the exposure is not great such a site may be ideal for a garden. The soil may be far better drained than that of low-land sites and, if they are south-facing, they will receive more sunlight than a lowland site. Moreover, the sun's rays will be concentrated over a smaller area, producing a warmer situation.

Because of the direction of the prevailing winds, rainfall is far greater on the west coast than on the east. The rainfall is greatest on the windward side of a range of hills and, providing the soil is well drained, this makes for lush growth and good crops. Valleys and other depressions receive the sun later, and do not benefit from the warm air currents, suffering from frost traps. Not only will they remain covered with frost well into the morning, when high or flatland areas nearby have cleared, but they will also experience frost

when adjacent lands remain an important one or two degrees above freezing point.

All other factors being equal, towns have a slightly higher temperature than the surrounding countryside. This is a result of the heat from the houses, and energy generated by industry and the internal combustion engine. All of these features relating to the exact location are even more important than the general area in which the garden is situated. It is these factors of the micro-climate that allow for the occasional reversal of the norm – for example, some delicate species can be grown in the north which would not survive in parts of the south. When you are considering the micro-climate, it is important that you take due account of all factors, and weigh up their general importance, if necessary plotting the effects upon a garden plan.

DRAINAGE

Before studying the possibilities of any garden it is important to consider the drainage of the site. This will not present a problem if you live on a hillside or you are taking over a well-established garden. It will be of considerable importance with level or lowland sites where, in the most

Fig 6 Any existing features should be examined carefully before finalising the design. Here the line of the stream is accentuated by the use of well-chosen plants.

extreme cases of bad drainage, the water table may rise above the surface. Sites with a clay pan which stops the water from running away will present similar problems in virtually any position. Plants need water, but, with most varieties, the roots also need to be able to breathe, and they will die if they are continually under water. The exceptions to these are bog and water plants, which have modified structures – for example, the stems of water lilies are honeycombed to provide a much larger surface area, allowing for a far more efficient exchange of the air dissolved in the water (rather like the gills of a fish). They also have modified leaves, depending upon whether they are above the water or whether they float on top of it.

The effect of frost is more pronounced and remains longer where there is a large excess of water. Successful over-wintering of the more delicate subjects lies as much with providing good drainage as with frost protection. Some plants (but not all) can survive the extremes of cold of all but our most severe winters, providing their roots are fairly dry. It is often the combined effect of the cold and excess water that is responsible for the loss of many half-hardy subjects during the winter. In addition, where there is poor drainage soils tend to become very sour with a low pH, and severe drainage problems must be overcome by the laying of land drainage pipes to a sump, if you are ever to produce a worthwhile garden.

CHAPTER 2

The Main Features

APPROACHES

Lancelot 'Capability' Brown, arguably the greatest British landscape gardener of all time, is said to have acquired his nickname from his habit of describing a new challenge as 'having capability'. Whilst we are not concerned with plots of the size of those with which he commonly dealt, nor are ever likely to have the opportunity to become involved with such areas, the principle remains the same. However small, awkwardly-shaped or unpromising at first appearance a site may be, every one must be recognised as having enormous potential. There can be beauty in a garden of any size, and each different size and shape should be approached in the most appropriate way. You should remember both that a small garden is not a miniature version of a large garden, and that a part of a large garden cannot successfully be transferred to a smaller urban plot. A window box can be a great delight, providing you realise and appreciate its limitations. The same rule applies to a garden. The only real restrictions on the development of your garden lie in your imagination.

The desire of recent years to utilise every piece of available urban land has led to ingenious approaches by architects, yielding ever-smaller and often irregularly-shaped plots. Sometimes, little thought is given to the landscaping of the site, and priority lies with achieving the maximum number of housing units. Neverthe-less, even the very small gardens attached to these housing units are, from a gardening standpoint, no more than variations on a theme, and unless the challenge of landscaping is met, the architectural potential of new housing will never be realised. Building land is encroaching ever further into the green belt, and it is the responsibility of each and every one of us to ensure that the country begins to come to the town. This is essential if we are to avoid a mass of concrete jungles.

The average house will have two plots, one at the front, which is part of the street scene, and the more secluded back plot – a house situated on a corner may be considered to possess two street scenes. Before becoming involved in approaching the design of a garden, it is necessary to appreciate the range of features that are available. It should be realised from the outset that the designer usually has quite a wide choice in terms of features, and that several of the alternatives are equally applicable to both front or back sites. The most important factor when you are planning a garden is *balance*. This is the satisfactory interaction of all of the component parts – the colour, form and shape of the organic elements (the plants), and of the inorganic elements (the house walls, the paths and any water features). Achieving balance does not imply providing the same amount of each element. Some factors, such as bright colours, have a more dramatic effect, and may need to be concentrated in just one area, while others must extend their influence throughout the garden.

THE FENCE

The fence has a symbolic role – that of defining the boundary of a property. It is useful to know

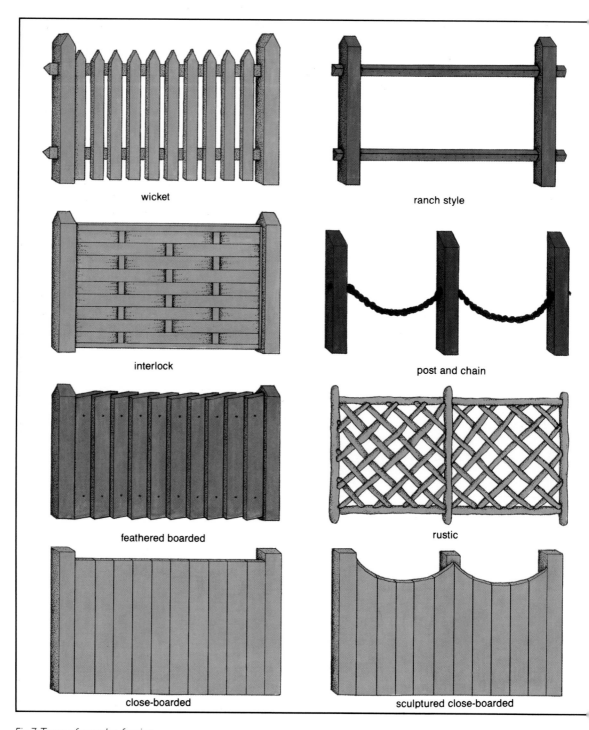

wicket

ranch style

interlock

post and chain

feathered boarded

rustic

close-boarded

sculptured close-boarded

Fig 7 Types of wooden fencing.

to whom the fence belongs and whose responsibility it is, therefore, to maintain it. Find out as soon as possible, in order to avoid problems later. A fence should not be thought of as a nuisance, or an unnecessary expense, but rather as a feature to enhance the garden, or the framework within which the landscape is created. As such, it warrants consideration as careful as that given to every tree or shrub.

Nothing looks worse, and few things can more effectively destroy the ambience of a garden, than a poor quality wooden fence. The interwoven larch type is just such a fence, which, although cheap, can be very prone to wind damage — sometimes the whole structure can be blown over — and to distortion of the individual laths. A fence in a state like this creates the impression of untidiness, and a garden that is poorly cared for, irrespective of the appearance of the rest of the plot. Another disadvantage of this type of fence is that you will be obliged to treat it regularly with a wood preservative if it is to maintain a decent appearance, and survive the ravages of the elements. The wooden supports are particularly prone to rotting at ground level, unless they are placed in metal casings to protect them. Overall, these fences are ugly, they are ineffective as wind breaks, and they are also liable to exclude too much sunlight. They are cheap and easy to erect, but you should consider carefully their visual impact a few years later.

Good quality wooden fences of a more solid construction, on the other hand, can make an

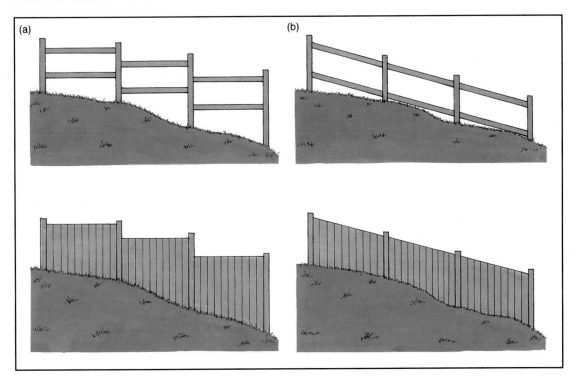

Fig 8 Fencing a sloping site. (a) The main fencing posts are set 6ft (2m) apart. The cross struts are screwed into position after the level has been set using a spirit level. The fencing of your choice is then attached to the frame. (b) Here the fence follows the general slope of the ground. The highest and lowest posts are positioned. The depth to which the intermediate posts are to be sunk is established by stretching a piece of string from the top of the first post to the top of the last.

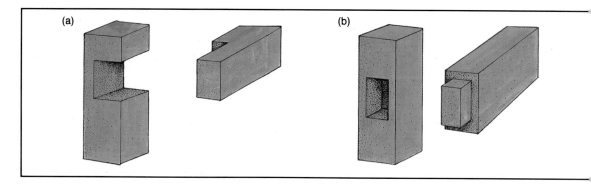

Fig 9 Fencing joints. (a) The open joint is best suited to lighter structures, in which the horizontal strut is much smaller than the upright. (b) The bayonet-type fitting should be used where strong horizontal supports are used in the structure.

important contribution to the appearance of a garden. It is relatively easy to include curves in them, and these can provide an interesting extra dimension to the design.

HEDGES

Hedges have much to commend them. They are the only organic boundaries available, and may provide greenery throughout the year, with copper beeches giving golden colours during the dark days of winter. Hedges can be made from virtually all shrubs. One good example is *forsythia*, one of the easiest and cheapest of all shrubs to grow – all you need to do is to break off a mature wood shoot with a 'boot' in the spring, summer or autumn, place it in a moist loamy soil, and wait for it to root. Rooted cuttings placed at 20in (50cm) intervals will soon form a dense screen which can be cut and trained into a hedge. A *forsythia* hedge will greet the spring with a bright, primrose-yellow show of flowers that will light up a street, and this will be followed by a mass of light green leaves. For a complete range of spring colour, *forsythia* is essential, and it will also be possible to use stems from your hedge in floral arrangements. Remember that it is always worth considering the alternative roles that

garden subjects can perform before making your final choice. *Forsythia* is in its element grown in a hedge, where it not only creates a boundary for your garden and lights up the street, but also becomes a source of cut stems for floral arrangement and, if you're lucky, provides a site for a bird to build its nest.

The range of shrubs which can be used in this way is almost limitless. For example, the camellia, another spring-flowering shrub, may be grown successfully as a hedge in even the smallest garden, instead of being planted in its more usual position as a major feature in a larger garden. Annual trimming means that this exotic subject from the Orient can easily be restricted to perfectly manageable proportions. Camellias will not dominate a small site as long as they are prevented from growing unchecked, which is the more common way of cultivating it. The shrubs can be found in shades of red, white and pink, and a mixed planting of varieties will make an even more interesting hedge. Camellias should be planted no closer than 3ft (1m) apart, at any time from November to February, in an acid soil. They will only die if there is any chalk present.

Other suitable shrub subjects include *Chaenomeles japonica* (*Moules japonica*) and *Escallonia* 'Apple Blossom', which will form a hedge of pinkish-white, flowering during early

June. Where the hedge is to form a backcloth for herbaceous or mixed beds, you can create a cottage-garden effect by planting a few metres of one type of shrub followed by a differing length of another. The range may be chosen to provide an interesting hedge throughout the majority of the year.

Another popular plant for hedging is Lawson's Cypress, which is one of the fastest growing of all evergreens in cultivation, and can be trained to any height you choose. Lawson's Cypress can also be allowed to grow into a tree – it will be statuesque, and really only suited to the largest urban and country gardens. The combined effect of its roots, and the shadow it casts, is that very little that is positioned under it will grow successfully, and as a result a large part of a small garden would be removed from cultivation. The species is useful to produce almost instant height in a conifer garden, but is not suitable for a rockery, unless you are prepared to dig it out and discard it regularly. This is a wasteful and expensive process, and its only alternative is to replant the shrub in another position where it can grow un-hindered. However, the dwarf versions of Lawson's Cypress – 'Nana' and 'Minima' – can be used for this purpose with some success.

Two plants you would do best to avoid are laurel and privet, hedging favourites of our grandparents. These gained their popularity because of their evergreen nature, but really they are the least interesting of hedging plants and to use them is to waste the opportunity that creating a hedge presents. Perhaps more than any others, these shrubs reflect the attitude of our near ancestors towards gardens and towards life itself, where neatness and order was all-important. Laurel and privet are in great contrast to, for example, yew. This is probably the oldest of all our decorative hedging materials and is often found in church-yards of great antiquity, but with its dense growth it is an evergreen that still sparkles with vitality. Yew lends itself to shaping and topiary far better than any other tree. (Incidentally, you

should be aware that topiary is not beyond anyone's ability, and is a distinctive feature of landscaping that might be considered by those who have the time and patience to train and trim the figures – even the simplest of geo-metrical shapes can give a garden a unique appearance. However, if you prefer, it is possible to buy partly-trained bushes from some garden centres.) Please remember that the disadvantage of yew is that it produces extremely poisonous red berries which could be tempting to young children. Only plant yew trees if you can be sure that little fingers will not be able to reach the fruit. If there is a danger of this, then an alternative to yew is box, another traditional topiary subject. Box is also ideal as a hedging plant, as a single specimen, or even for patio pot culture.

Also increasing in popularity as hedging materials are the *rosa* species, such as *Rosa rugosa*, which can be successfully used to make a dense hedge. In addition to its flowers with their typical rose perfume, this plant produces bright-coloured hips in the autumn – these can be harvested and the vitamin C (in which they are very rich) extracted. *Rosa rugosa* makes an ideal fence where it is necessary to keep out intruders, such as dogs.

Training a shrub to form a hedge usually involves no more than planting the plants reasonably close together, typically 18in–3ft (½–1m) apart. You will not need to attempt to weave half-chopped branches in the manner of a countryman making an animal-proof fence!

WALLS

In addition to providing an external boundary, walls may be required to separate parts of the garden – one example of this is terracing (*see* page 26). They may be built from bricks, large pieces of stone (such as flint, or quarried stone like Portland, Purbeck or Cotswold), or dressed slabs. It is also possible to obtain artificial and reconstituted weathered materials, and these

Fig 10 (above) The construction of a well – a dry stone wall, a cemented stone wall and a rock garden are all present in this corner of a cottage garden.

Fig 11 (below) The same garden – a view showing the cottage and the position of the wall.

can be equally suitable from an aesthetic point of view. Whilst hedges and fencing will probably need to be replaced from time to time, walls are far more permanent and it is ideal, therefore, that they should all be made at the same time of a harmonious style and materials. Where a house has bricks of a particular type and colour it is important that any walling material should be matching or complementary, as a brick of a different type will give the impression of a piece-meal job. Remember that the garden should blend with the house, and that you should be thinking in terms of an overall exterior decoration. Gardens and houses are less and less considered to be distinct entities but rather are coming to be thought of as component parts of the whole.

It is insufficient simply to ensure that the walling material matches the house. As a garden designer you should look beyond your own boundaries to the area as a whole, and where either brick or stone is to be used, thought must be given to the style of the neighbourhood – this is particularly important where the area has a distinct and recognisable character. Where a house is rendered, it is possible to use any type or colour of brick. With the older type of rendered property, stonework can produce some desirable effects, but serious thought is needed before using weathered stone in ultra-modern properties – in many of the present-day developments the open patio-type blocks would be far better suited to the surroundings. Stone has an eternal quality about it, and, whilst this can be used to good effect, in the wrong place it will 'clash' and only serve to emphasise the

Fig 12 The open patio block wall serves as a formal division within the garden, and the two levels inherent in this particular design provide for further division as well as giving the illusion of both increased mass and size. Container-grown plants at the side of the slope serve to break up the starkness of the barrier.

difference between the natural and modern man-made materials. Since stone walls in most districts are associated with old houses, incorporating stone into the landscaping of a 1980s house will give the effect of a diversity of styles. This in turn creates the impression that the whole urban environment is unplanned. However, stone *can* be used in rock gardens in such areas, as it then serves the same purpose as a bright contrasting colour, emphasising a feature, or acting as a focal point.

Retaining Walls

Where land is sloping, as landscape designer you have two possible choices. You can either work with the slopes and just perform levelling operations in terms of that slope, rather than trying to create a flat character, or, alternatively, you may create terracing. Terracing is invariably the better approach, especially in the smaller garden, with the variation in level creating extra interest. With completely flat sites, too, serious consideration should be given to artificially creating two levels by movement of soil. Whilst this does not of course yield any extra space, it does give the impression that a positive design for the whole area has been achieved.

If you decide on terracing you will need to build retaining walls capable of withstanding the pressure resulting from the weight of the soil pushing against them. To provide this strength (especially where the dry walling technique is adopted) you must build your wall with a batter – that is, a slope receding from the ground upwards. The slope need only be very slight – 5–15 degrees – a greater deviation is unnecessary and it will appear contrived. Also, you should always make it clear to a brick supplier that you need materials that are capable of withstanding the forces to which they will be subjected – only the strongest bricks will perform the task satisfactorily.

When building a conventional wall, with mortar between the joints, it is a good idea to break some of the bricks in half, leaving a few half

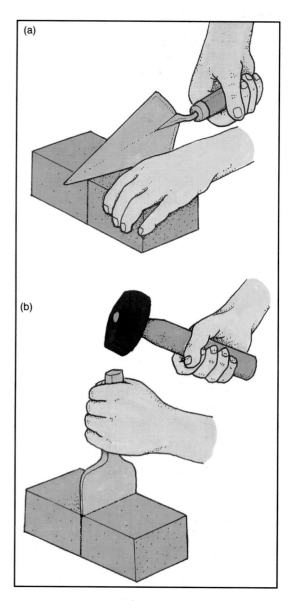

Fig 13 Cutting bricks. (a) Make a groove above the brick with a broad blade. (b) Break the brick by placing the chisel in the groove and giving it a few sharp blows with a bricklayer's hammer.

spaces empty. You can then fill the gaps that are left with good quality loam, and plant them with trailing bedding plants. *Alyssum, aubrieta* and *lobelia* will all make the wall come alive. When

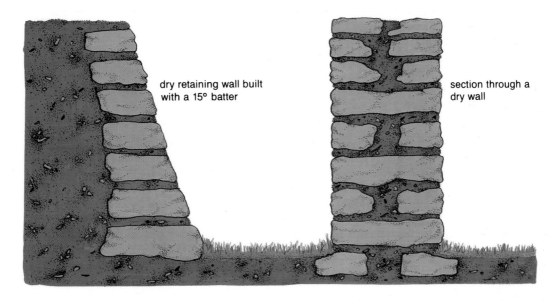

dry retaining wall built
with a 15° batter

section through a
dry wall

Fig 14 Dry walls.

you are planting a dry wall the same rules apply as for beds, and you should put the plants in groups, having regard for the season in which they flower. For example, if you plant *aubrieta* on its own it will last for just a month, contributing only pale green leaves throughout the rest of the year. A carefully chosen selection will ensure that the wall retains an interesting appearance for months on end.

Free-Standing Walls

Unlike a retaining wall, a free-standing wall should not be built with a batter, but should consist of two walls about 10in (25cm) apart. Broken brick or another drainage material can be placed into the space between the walls, while the top third can be filled with a good loam and gravel mix, and planted with trailing subjects, or other suitable bedding material. Ideal plants include antirrhinums, violas, pansies and *tagetes*. Walls to be planted should be considered as vertical flower beds and treated accordingly. Correctly constructed they provide a good aspect, satisfactory drainage, and the advantage that the stonework will retain a thin layer of moisture similar to a rock garden. Alpines can be very successfully grown on walls as the difference between a stone wall and a rock garden created on a slope is only a matter of degree.

Trellis Work

Trellis work provides the support for various plants and its main visual impact is in the vertical plane – the screen formed serving to separate off parts of the garden. However, it does not itself provide any effective protection against the wind and should never be used for an external boundary. When plants are trained over a wall it is usual to leave much of the wall visible, with the plants adding to the character. With trellis work the opposite applies – that is, the aim is to hide as much of the wooden structure as is possible as it is only providing a support for the plants. Trellis work can be used as a screen between various styles of garden, but more commonly it is used to partition off functional areas containing the shed, greenhouse and compost heap, or the area where the dustbins, washing lines and even the

Fig 15 This wrought iron arch and fencing effectively divides areas of the garden without being too intrusive.

car are kept. It can give the impression of solitude and privacy – two features that many people wish to create in their garden – yet at the same time it does not give the sense of claustrophobia that comes with more substantial structures.

Rural gardeners used to make a far more open structure than the lath trellis work of the urban areas, relying on poles, often of larch. This may well be considered as an integral part of the cottage garden, where the screen itself is a feature in its own right. When trellis work is first made from larch with the bark retained it is a joy to the eye, but the outer covering soon disintegrates. The poles are attacked by insects such as wood-lice and suffer the ravages of rot caused as a result of wood-consuming fungi prospering in wet weather. The result of this is

that a structure that is secure in the summer may not survive the ravages of autumn's gales. Joint construction is extremely important, if you are to avoid the problems of the poles splitting. Wood preservatives do afford a degree of protection, but take care to use one of the modern green or brown shades, which will blend in with the surroundings, and avoid the older type of creosote.

It is far safer to build your structure from planed wood. Wood from a demolition site or a dealer in second-hand timber is perfectly adequate, and very much cheaper than new timber. Holes from which nails have been removed may be filled in with putty, and will be unnoticeable once the structure has been erected and treated with preservative. A minimum size of 2 x 2in (5 x 5cm) must be used for the main frame. One mistake that is often made with trellis work is having too few uprights – you should place an upright every 3ft (1m) along the structure, and on exposed sites further support in the form of diagonal struts below the meshwork should be provided. Finally, nail the meshwork into position. Made in this way, and with regular attention, your trellis will last for several years.

The ideal use for the trellis is to produce a crop of roses. Today there is a vast range of colours available, and roses must be the most suitable flowers for such locations; with 'dead-heading' it is possible to have a profusion of blooms from June right through to the autumn frosts. Other subjects, such as the clematis, can also be used, but their flowering periods are far shorter. You should never mix species, but do experiment with colour combinations of different hybrids. Decide whether you wish the screen to attract the eye or whether you are seeking a blending effect, with the screen merging into the background. Clematis (especially the *Jackmanii* hybrids) is particularly suited to providing the selections of harmonious colour that are needed for the latter approach, but trellis used in this way is not at its most effective – it tends to suffer in that it only provides colour in the vertical plane. A far better approach is to encourage the eye to move up from a bed planted at the base of the screen. To do this, build the framework up to 6ft (2m), but only put in the meshwork from 3ft (1m) upwards. Use the area below to plant selected herbaceous subjects which will grow from 2–3ft (up to 1m). Choose perennials such as lupins, stocks, delphinium and flag irises – these are all ideal as they tend to come into flower in the late spring or early summer, with the trellis subjects taking over at a later date. In this way, you will have continuous colour. More importantly, their spike-like flowers will tend to lead the eye upwards. An annual bed which comes into flower at almost the same time as those on the trellis may be used, but do choose the annuals with care as the tendency with modern hybrids is to produce colours that are as bright and dazzling as possible. When considering the colour of a screen, remember that it will only need to blend in on its own terms as the observer will not usually be able to see beyond the barrier that it forms.

In the garden which has to perform a function as well as being decorative, the screen itself provides valuable growing space for subjects such as cordon fruit trees trained diagonally along wires. Trees cultivated in such a way will tend to sterilise far less land than a normal fruit tree of spreading growth, and such screens should not be dismissed lightly, even where fruit production is not a primary consideration. They will be a thing of beauty in their own right, with a spring bouquet of apple blossom, followed by the leaves making up the screen in the summer months, and turning to gold in the autumn. A border of herbaceous evergreen subjects planted at the base of such a screen will effectively take over the role during the months when the trees are bare. Support for cordon trees is best made from mild steel piping 1in (25mm) in diameter, with holes bored at approximately 12in (30cm) intervals, to take 1mm wire. The wires must be pulled taut with pliers and fastened to the poles. Whether they are wooden or metal (this should be painted a matt green shade), it is necessary to treat all structures thoroughly before any planting takes place – it may be impossible to paint them once the trees have become established. As is the case with every other feature of the garden, walls and fences must harmonise or contrast with the design as a whole. In far too many layouts they serve at best as a contrast, and at worse no consideration at all is given to their position in relationship to the whole, resulting in an unbalanced appearance. The wall may be an extension of a rock garden where the vertical is a natural progression of the horizontal, in the same way that a yew hedge can be grown as an extension of another great mass of green – the lawn.

Fig 16 (a) A garden which may be enclosed or open plan. It allows for the growing of trees, both perennials and annuals, yet the replacement of grass by paving reduces the amount of attention required. (b) An enclosed garden, suitable for a small town house – again requiring the minimum amount of maintenance. Choice of trees is very important – they should not exceed 10ft (3m) and should provide flowers in the spring and coloured buds during the autumn.

Fig 17 A small pergola suitable for confined spaces to which hanging baskets have been added. These provide a spectacular display of colour, while the climbers have been planted so that eventually they will meet to give an archway effect.

PERGOLA

These garden features, based on aspects of Far-Eastern garden design, were once very popular. They did suffer a reversal in their fortunes, but are now enjoying a revival. The pergola consists of a wooden archway or covered path, made of an upright trellis-type framework. The two sides are joined by battens across the top, to form an arch structure. The pergola is a three-dimensional trellis, which you may walk through, and where, on a hot summer's day, you may enjoy the shade from a deck chair, bathing in the seductive perfume of the flowers which make up the living part of the structure. Pergolas are also ideal for *al fresco* dining – far superior to simply sitting out in the open. For a pergola to be used in this way, it should ideally be at least 10ft (3m) wide, but greater width is not a problem as long as space allows, and the only extra expense will be the longer length of battens across the top. Wide areas produced in this way provide the ultimate in privacy. Whilst still enjoyable,

narrower pergolas tend to be restrictive. Where it is intended that the structure should function only as a walkway, it should be at least 6ft (2m) in width.

As with all features in a garden, a pergola must serve a specific purpose. In design terms, garden features will not 'work' unless they are an integral part of the whole scheme, so your trellis framework ideally should lead the walker to a place of interest. A pergola is essentially a connecting corridor, and as such it should lead from one garden to another, or, extended, from a gateway to a garage, for example. It could be constructed to lead from the front garden to the back garden, but you must give careful thought to the effect that this will have on the door. At worst it will shower any visitor with raindrops during a storm, at best the door will be in permanent shade. Usually it is far better in such a situation to rely on a climber rose outside the door, which will create the desired illusion equally well.

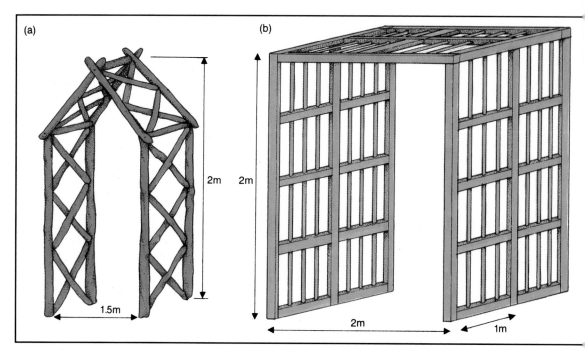

(a)

(b)

2m

2m

1.5m

2m

1m

Fig 18 (a) A rustic archway, which may be used to support a climber rose. Even the smallest site can find room for some three-dimensional wooden garden structure. Over the front gate is the most obvious position, but sites will abound throughout the garden. (b) Section through a pergola. This structure, made from planed wood, may be planted with sweet-smelling prolific-flowering species.

PATHS AND DRIVES

A path is far more than just an area to walk on – it leads the eye of the stationary observer slavishly to its conclusion, thereby picking out and defining a focal point in the garden. Gentle curves used in the garden will cause the eye to dwell longer, and this delay will give the impression that the garden is far longer than it really is. Mystery can be created by a curve simply leading behind a protruding border of high shrubs, or to a point behind a trellis work or hedge. Nothing can create the illusion of mystery and suspense quite in the same way as the humble path.

The first decision to make is where a path would be desirable – although it does have a purely artistic merit, it must, like the pergola, lead from one part of the garden to another. If you intend to create a garden feature around a lawn, then a path is not necessary. Lawns, even those of high quality containing no rye grass in their composition, will take quite a lot of wear (as can be seen from a bowling green). What they will not tolerate, however, is rough-soled shoes or wheelbarrows. If a pathway is essential for a wheelbarrow, but you do not wish to accentuate it, site it down the side of the garden. This can turn out to be quite economical in terms of space, if you construct your path below a hedge, which will effectively have sterilised the soil in its immediate vicinity anyway. At all costs, you should avoid siting such a path in an area that is bathed either in the morning or midday sun – not only will the path be highlighted by the sun, but such an area will also be a prime growing site and, as such, would be better reserved for bedding plants.

Where a path is to be a feature in its own right, it should never be constructed down the centre of the plot. Rather than creating a balance, this actually destroys it. A garden is a picture, in the same way as a painting or a photograph, and the

Fig 19 Paths and paved areas can be used to create features in their own right as in this attractive brick design.

principles of composition must apply to its design just as they do to any other work of art. The most important of these principles is the two-thirds rule. This says that the main features should not be half-way across or down the garden, but that they should have a one-third, two-thirds relationship to the boundary. This implies dividing the garden into two sections, in either direction, one approximately twice the length of the other, to create an overall balance (providing the two sections complement each other).

With a new garden, in which virtually no construction work has been done, the designer has a definite advantage — not only is he able to choose his own type of pathing materials, but he may also situate the gate in the position of his choice. Because a path in a front garden necessarily serves a specific purpose, its starting point, the gate, and its destination, the door, are fixed. Of course, you have no control over the position of the door, but you are free to site the gate anywhere you like. Where the door lies in

the centre of the house front it is far better to allow the path to sweep diagonally towards it, thereby dividing the garden into one-third and two-third sections, than simply running a straight path at ninety degrees to the street. If the door is situated to one side of the house, it is still possible to split the garden into a smaller and a larger plot, and pleasing effects may be produced with a combination of herbaceous and shrub borders or rockery and water gardens.

If both the gate and the door lie in the centre of their respective structures, the framework is established for a formal geometrical garden. The best way to view the plot is as a whole, with one half presenting the mirror image of the other, rather than as two component complementary parts. Many modern properties are built complete with a drive, with the path to the door as a natural extension, leaving one space where the garden is to be made. Even where the drive is fixed by the relative positions of the gate and the garage, the choice of the position of the feeder path does still lie with the owner, and he need not be dictated to by the preconceived ideas of the builder or a previous resident.

The smaller plots of the modern urban estate are such that it is possible to design a garden without constructing a path, and it is tempting to feel that if you omit this feature, your plot will appear to be bigger with a more open aspect. You will, however, almost certainly feel the need for a path once you try to manage your garden, and without a path the garden will seem to lack a purpose, taking on the visual characteristics of an open field. With a reasonably large garden you may effectively use paths to create a series of gardens with an open-plan layout, and you will need no three-dimensional structures to separate the various parts of the garden.

Unfortunately, generalisations cannot be made when it comes to irregular shaped plots, such as a garden on a corner. Here again the principle of division by hedges, screens and paths should be adopted, but you should try to avoid *artificially* splitting a corner plot into two. If it will not 'work', it is better to develop it as a single garden

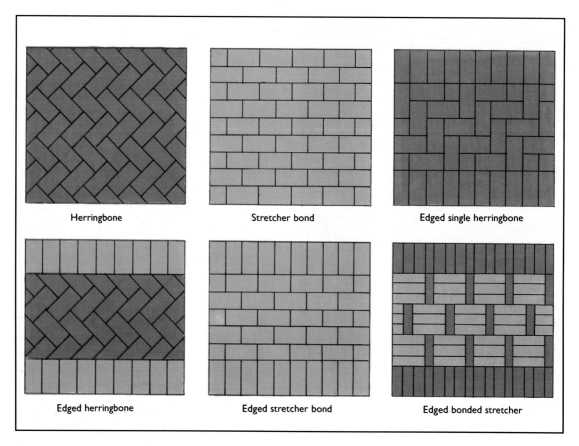

Fig 20 Styles of paths and bricked areas.

possessing a common theme throughout, or allow the styles to change within it, as they do in a long plot. An irregular space should be seen as an opportunity to be exploited, and not as an inconvenience

The walls and hedges are the framework of the garden and the path system is its skeleton, and all items will radiate from this. No matter how carefully features are devised and how painstakingly the plants are selected, unless the paths are correctly sited and constructed, your garden will never realise its full potential. This should not discourage you from using paths as a feature in their own right, and you should never try to hide a path – it may be functional but it need not be unsightly. The path is an integral part, so it does not necessarily have to be narrow; this is one of the commonest mistakes. A narrow path, with its sharp edges, produces a

far greater contrast than a wide drive, which will merge into the landscape far more readily. A very large drive can be a feature in itself and, if it is used in conjunction with the curves of beds and lawns, the amount of essential maintenance work will be greatly reduced, while at the same time the garden will retain sufficent character to ensure that it keeps its 'designed' look. Very wide paths that do not have to act as drives may be broken up by a bed, and this can be as simple or as complex as you wish. The larger the bed, the better. If it is sufficently large it will effectively divide the driveway into two.

Siting a planting area in the middle of a path offers one of the best opportunities for the construction of a raised bed. This type of bed is ideal not only for the handicapped gardener, but also (with its counterpart, the sunken garden) to add an extra dimension to any landscape. The

Fig 21 A well-designed path can add to the overall atmosphere as in this cottage garden.

raised garden has one major advantage – in terms of soil it is a completely controlled environment, and it is therefore far easier to create the perfect growing medium. This should be rich in nutrients, together with water-retaining humus, yet kept open to provide the drainage.

The construction of a path will depend upon the architectural characteristics already present, as well as on the materials that are available. For example, before considering a stone path (for which sheets of partially-dressed stone will be required), check what is available in the locality, as transport costs can be extremely high. A stone path offers the greatest opportunity of all to create a natural-looking environment. To give the impression of order it may be laid out with the straight part of the stone making up the sides. Much of the success of this type of path will depend upon having a sufficiently large number of pieces to choose from, and these must be fitted inside the path framework in a jigsaw pattern, with the gaps being filled up with concrete made from five parts sand to two parts

cement. Try to make the 'joints' between the pieces of stone as small as possible and of the same thickness. You should avoid having large areas of concrete to fill in awkward places – break a slab of stone with a chisel until you obtain a piece of the correct size and shape.

In the cottage-type garden it is more usual to lay a path without cementing the pieces together. The gaps will act as an oasis, receiving all the water that runs off the path, washing down the seeds that fall on to the stones. In between the gaps many plants will germinate – several will be weeds, which will need to be pulled up, whilst others can be allowed to develop into points of interest.

Bricks can often be purchased in small quantities (of about one to two thousand) relatively cheap, and those that have to survive as a path must have a fair degree of mechanical strength. Brick paths may be laid in a variety of different patterns, and you may choose either to place cement or sand in the gaps. If you wish to avoid weeding between the blocks, then the area may be treated with a weedkiller.

A natural material that can be used to good effect for a path is slices through a tree trunk. You will require hardwood pieces at least 4–6in (10–15cm) thick, which have been thoroughly treated with preservative before. Bury them until they are flush with the lawn, allowing a gap of 6–8in (15–20cm) between each portion of trunk. Before laying a trunk path always remove the bark – this has little strength and also tends to harbour the parasites which attack and destroy timber. Pieces of stone, too, may be placed in a lawn in a similar sort of way. Whether you are using pieces of wood or stone it will be much easier to cut your lawn if you have a hover mower. It is important that you consider aspects such as this when you are planning your garden features – wood or stone paths are totally impractical where a formal lawn mown in strips is required.

Load-bearing drives that may function as parking spaces can be made of tarmac, or concrete, although the latter very quickly shows

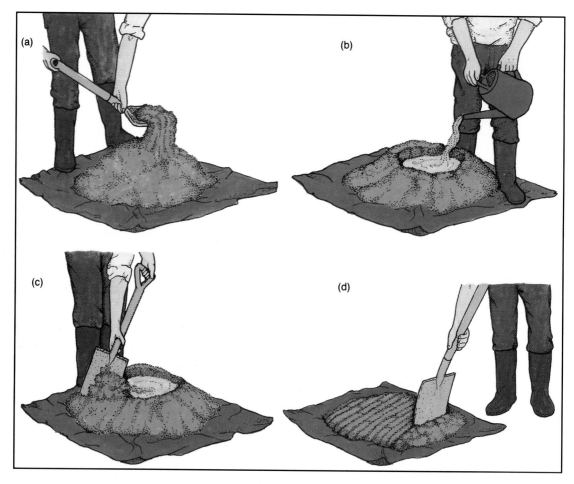

Fig 22 Mixing cement. There are two main cement mixes used in construction work – one part cement to three part sharp sand for all bonding work, and two parts cement to five parts sand for structural work such as paths. (a) Place a large sheet of plastic on the ground and mix up your elements in a heap. (b) Create a depression to make a volcano shape. Add water until the dip is one-third full. With the spade, work the mixture into the water. (c) Work in the solid until there is no water remaining. Make another depression and add more water. Repeat the process until the cement has the consistency of toothpaste. (d) To ensure even and thorough mixing move the spade across the heap in a series of 'chopping' actions. (For very large areas it will pay you to consider purchasing ready-made concrete.)

all signs of dirt, cracks and deteriorates in other ways rather than improving with keeping. Such drives present few problems in terms of maintenance, but they do tend to be rather uninteresting. This can be relieved by the inclusion of bowls or tubs which can be filled with spring bulbs and then summer bedding plants. The wide drive is an open space similar to that formed by a patio, and the garden designer should treat it accordingly. Styles of gardening are not absolute – they are a guide to help the landscaper, not a set of rules to be rigidly adhered to. The load-bearing area will function as a drive, yet it can successfully retain several of the characteristics of a patio, and may be treated as such with hanging baskets, urns and the rest of

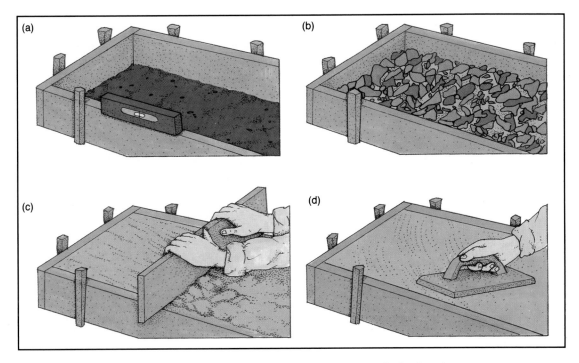

Fig 23 Constructing a concrete path. (a) Excavate the soil to a depth of 4–6in (10–15cm), and construct shuttering level with the top of the path (use a spirit level). The boards should be held in position with wooden pegs which can be hammered flush when the boards are level. (b) Fill with broken brick and other hardcore to a depth of 2–3in (5–7.5cm) from the top. Give a light spraying of water from a can. (c) Fill with concrete to about level with the shuttering. Find a piece of timber with a flat edge, and, with arms outstretched, use it to smooth off the path, pulling it towards you with a zig-zag motion. (d) Achieve a really smooth surface by rubbing with a wooden bricklayer's float.

the paraphernalia of the Spanish courtyard. One point which is often not appreciated is that plants in a border next to a driveway prosper far better than those grown beside a lawn. The reason for this is the combined effect of the extra water which runs off the surface and the water retention effect of the underside of the stone. This can be particularly important if you intend being away from home for some time during the summer, or if you cannot water regularly for some other reason. Planting in such a position will go some way towards protecting the more water-dependent subjects, such as the summer bedding plants with their comparatively small roots, but it will only prove useful for a limited period of time.

STEPS

Steps are another feature which will create the illusion of moving from one garden to another without involving a large amount of space. They can also accentuate a change in levels, which need not be great – you will find that 4in (10cm) is sufficient height change between each step, with the steps themselves 18in (45cm) deep (this includes a 2in (5cm) overlay). Where there is sufficient room, external steps which spread beyond the path and the retaining wall should be constructed. This will give the impression of spaciousness, in the same way as it would inside a large house. However, steps should be apparent without being dominant, so it would

37

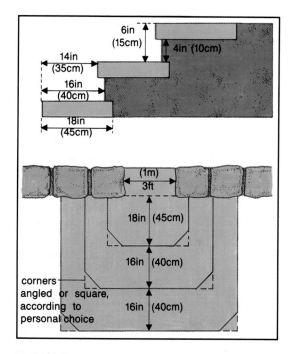

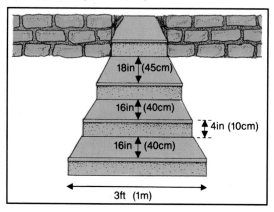

Fig 24 (a) Planning external steps.

(b) Planning internal steps.

Fig 25 The herbaceous border alongside a stone path.

not work to use this approach in a very small area. Here the steps should be confined within walls that are at least 3ft (lm) apart, with the wall being built beside the steps. Choice of material is extremely important, and it should be the same as that of the retaining walls and the rest of the garden architecture.

CHAPTER 3

The First Steps

BEFORE YOU DO ANYTHING

Before you embark on any gardening scheme it is essential that you realise how you wish the finished garden to look. This does not mean that you cannot build your garden by instalments – you can, but only if you have planned it all beforehand. You must decide what features you want from the outset. Many gardens are neat in the sense that the lawns are cut, the beds are weed-free and the bushes are pruned, and individual beds may even have been planned or at least have had their finished format sketched on a piece of paper, but, taken as a whole, the garden may be a jumble of ideas with no cohesion to them. This is the inevitable consequence of starting work without an overall plan. You must be able to see the total concept in your mind's eye before a single sod is turned.

Your first step is to decide which features are most important to you, your family and your lifestyle; then decide upon your favourite plants and the role that the garden has to fulfil. The items that must be considered before you actually reach the stage of producing a plan include:

1. How large is the plot? Realise all of the possibilities and the limitations.
2. What are the natural features of the plot – is it flat or on a slope; is it dry land or wet land; is it exposed or sheltered?
3. How much time do you wish to spend in the garden maintaining it? Do you wish to reduce this to a minimum or is it going to become an important part of your life?
4. How much money is available to spend upon the garden? Gardening is a multi-million pound industry, and there are ways to make all tasks simpler, and plants and items to suit all tastes – at a price! It *is* possible to create an almost 'instant' garden, by placing out plants bought in their prime and replacing them when they have served their purpose, but the cost is liable to be completely unreasonable. You may think it is impossible to produce a designer landscape without spending a fortune, but this is not the case. You may propagate virtually all your own plants at minimal cost, and there are other ways of effecting savings such as planting trees and shrubs during the dormant season rather than purchasing the more expensive container-grown specimens that can be planted out at any time of

Fig 26 Permanent features such as paving, rockeries and ponds should be carefully thought out in the planning process. You will probably have to live with them for a few years, so it is best to get them right from the beginning.

Fig 27 A patio can have many uses in garden design. It reduces maintenance work and provides a
pleasant environment for dining outside or for children to play on. Container plants add colour and
break up the hard lines of the stonework.

the year. Container-grown plants *do* have their
uses — the building of the garden can take many
months and it may be advantageous to plant
some trees and bushes during the summer to
provide the necessary continuity in the work,
saving a year's growing time. Where bedding
plants and other plants that need replacing each
season are to be used, it will be necessary to
include a greenhouse in the overall layout to
avoid high on-going expenses.

5.   Do you wish the garden to remain the same
throughout the year, with only the seasonal
change of the individual permanent plants
altering, or do you wish to change the displays
with the seasons?

6.   Do you wish to grow a crop in the garden?
Whilst vegetables are not grown as much as they
once were, with the increased interest in
organically-grown foods there may be a return to
this type of gardening. If you see yourself as a
would-be back garden farmer you should give
serious thought to renting an allotment, which

can be done at a very modest cost. Fruit can be
grown in even the smallest gardens thanks to
modern root-stocks which dwarf the growth of
the tree. Alternatively, there are well-established
methods of growing trees along walls, and these
often produce the finest crops of all. Blooms for
the house may well be incorporated into any
scheme, providing that you choose the 'cut and
come again' species such as dahlia or sweet pea.

7.   Will the garden have to work in other ways?
Will you want it to provide dining-out areas and
play areas for children?

8.   Do you have any favourite features? You must
decide from the outset which features you wish
to incorporate in the garden. Ponds, rockeries
and herbaceous borders are all contenders for
space, and subjects such as sundials and
statuettes can be considered as focal points. It is
not possible to mix styles unless you decide to
divide the garden into a series of screened-off
sections. This will only work if the plot is of
sufficient size and it will also tend to be labour-

intensive. Do not fall into the trap of overcrowding. If you reduce the size of each section, trying to fit several styles into the space available, the reduced space will probably mean that none of the ideas will work.

9.   Do you intend to do the work yourself or will you employ a landscape gardener? Even if you do employ assistance you should be in control of the situation at all stages. There are many landscape gardeners who are good, and who will give you a successful plan, with useful suggestions as to how your own ideas can be put into practice. Unfortunately, there are also professionals of limited imagination and ability, who will try to force their views on how the garden should be developed. Remember, they may be more concerned with their profit margins than with your garden. The size and shape of a pond or the creation of a rockery all allow for a very profitable mark-up, and this may be their first consideration. There is no foolproof way of ensuring that anyone you employ is absolutely reliable, but a good workman should have no objection to providing you with a list of his previous customers to whom you can telephone for recommendations.

10.   Can you do manual work at present and will you be able to in the foreseeable future? Gardening should be a pleasure not a chore.

11.   What degree of permanence do you wish the features to possess? It is said that both pears and walnuts are planted for our grandchildren, but such features may be considered out of place in a time when we all have a far greater degree of mobility. It has also been suggested that some modern homes have only been designed to last for about sixty years, so that trees which take this long to reach maturity may be unsuitable. It must be realised that many schemes will take about three to five years to reach fruition. If you and your family will not be staying in one place for even this period of time, you should be thinking of ways to produce an instant garden. You could lay turves with bright summer bedding plants, and that way the plot will be at its best when you seek to sell the house.

THE SITE PLAN

By this stage you should be certain of the style of garden that you wish to create. The next task is to prepare a plan of the garden, and for this you should seek to use a scale of 1:100; not only is this a convenient size, but it will make light work of any calculations that are necessary. Using some graph paper marked out in 1cm grid, with one space corresponding to a metre, draw an accurate plan of the house, situated in the correct position on the whole site. Take care – any error at this stage will lead to incorrect plot and margin sizes which could cause confusion. Some features may appear to have sufficient room on the plan but will be far too small when they are actually built. The most practical way of measuring the size of a plot or feature is by making a marking string. Tie the end of a ball of string to a peg and mark it off at 3ft (1m) lengths, either using bits of coloured string or with a felt-tip pen. Work from the house or the wall, creating both a north–south and an east–west base line, and measure out the areas. Place stakes in the ground where you wish your design features to be sited, and then join up the stakes with coloured tape to mark out these features. Other important considerations, such as areas of near permanent sunlight or shade, can also be marked out. This is effectively the only realistic way of seeing the plan in life size before you are permanently committed to it.

Include in the basic plan all those features that are already on-site that you wish (or are forced) to retain, such as a garden shed, tree or tree trunk that you are unable to remove. This latter could be used for a clematis, or some other subject which requires that type of support. Once you have produced your plan, photocopy so that you have several spare sheets to work on; you will find that you can not have too many blank plans.

It is possible to design a garden using a computer, and this has advantages for the professional who has several commissions to consider. Much as we have come to rely on these

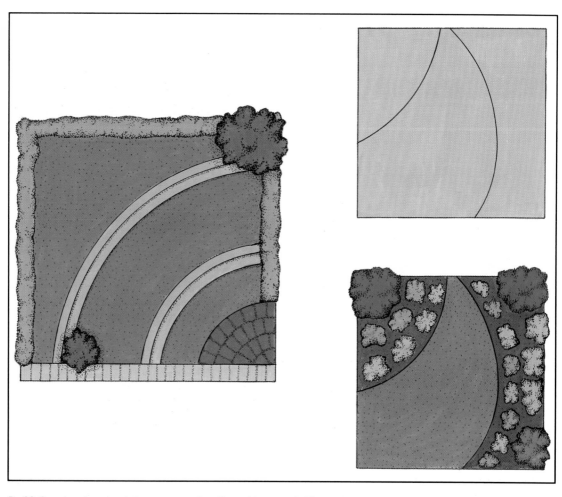

Fig 28 Creating three levels in a town garden. By making use of different levels, an impression of space can be created in a small garden. This technique is particularly useful with a square or almost square plot. (Note the bold use of curves to offset the geometrical design, and to provide mystery to suggest that the garden is bigger than it really is.)

aids, they are not capable of original thought or creativity, and can only suggest and move around those features that are fed into them. As such they are of very little use to the person who is simply seeking to plan his own garden. Yet there is no reason why, when looking for inspiration, you should not make use of the modern psychological technique of 'brain storming' – simply put down the first thoughts that enter your head on to one of the blank garden plans. Sit where you consider you have the most important view of the garden and draw in the features that you fancy. Nothing need be omitted at this stage. Simply attempt to plan the garden

without considering any of the constraints. By starting in this way you are sure to include the features that you really want in the completed garden. The danger with other approaches is that you may end up with a well-designed garden which does not, however, give you the pleasure you seek, since it does not contain certain plants that you might desire.

The View from the House

Once you have produced the basic sets of ideas they must be modified, as you progress from fanciful pipe dreams to the practicalities of

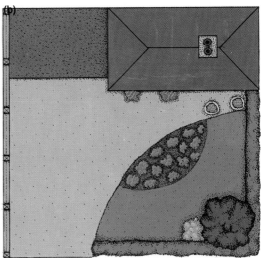

Fig 29 (a) A poor design for a small front garden. The tree planted near to the house will probably cause problems with its roots, as well as cutting out light to the house. It may prove difficult to get permission to remove the tree once it is fully developed. Also, the time-consuming border beds and central camellia give the impression of overcrowding. (b) A good design for a small front garden, with the tree planted away from the house, where it will not create problems, and will also enhance the street scene. The semi-shade tolerant camellia is planted near it. An alpine or heather garden is built near to the house, and the drive is enlarged, giving a more open character. Hanging baskets and urns are provided for extra bright colour.

garden design and maintenance. You should appreciate from the outset that the view from the various vantage points, and not the view from within the garden, should be the governing factor in design. It is surprising how little time you will spend actually in the garden just enjoying it – there are very few days which are warm enough for basking, or eating *al fresco*. Compare this with the hours you spend inside during the year and the significance of the external view becomes apparent. For gardens that are not contributing to the street scene, the view from the sitting room will be the most important. Where you have a room that faces on to the street, you will have to decide which is more important – the view from your window or from the streets. A garden which is well designed and maintained will always be a joy to its creator and also to the person who walks down the road – it is simply the focal points which will differ

according to your decision. It is possible to design the garden in such a way that both views are totally catered for, providing you appreciate the problem from the beginning. If in doubt, the golden rule must be to plan with regard to the view from the inside of your own property.

More Considerations

After your 'brain storming' session, put your plans away for a few days, quelling your urge to get on with the work. At this stage, take stock – remember that the garden may have to last you for several years, possibly the rest of your life, with only a few modifications to the original form, so it is unwise to rush the important design stage. Study the gardens around you; note the features which you like, and, just as importantly, those which you do not like, which must be avoided at all costs. No one would wish to copy

43

Fig 30 (a) Plot out the garden with any features that you wish to retain. The basic shape of the beds may be included at this stage. (b) The finished garden. Note the use of beds to hide the vegetable and service area from view.

another garden exactly, but there is no reason why you should not see how various features are integrated with each other. Discover from observation the relative sizes which work best. The gardens around your neighbourhood will probably be of a similar size and age to yours, and these are two important factors in garden design. They will also have broadly similar soil and meteorological conditions to contend with. Note the species which thrive. Judge your own street scene – is there a move to include subjects such as flowering cherries? Would the inclusion of one in your garden represent an important contribution to the road as a whole? Remember that garden design can be a matter of good neighbourliness. Once you are armed with an idea of what is possible, and current trends – another important factor to be considered in design, especially if you are going to sell the property in the near future and you wish to maximise your investment – go back to your original plan. Decide if there is anything you wish to change. There may be nothing, a few minor alterations may be necessary, or you may wish to discard the plan completely and start all over again.

ANALYSIS

An idea that works on paper and in the mind's eye may not necessarily be easily accomplished on your particular plot. Once again you must return to the drawing board, this time using a plan showing the areas of the garden which have the most and the least sunlight (not forgetting the effect of hedges, both in terms of excluding light, and of preventing growth underneath them). It is easier to use an overlay technique at this stage, using transparent plans drawn on acetate sheets. If you have access to an overhead projector, this will make the presentation and study of your plans much easier, but it is by no means essential. By now you should have put together a master plan, showing the view from the main room in the house, together with the light and dark areas.

If there is a pronounced slope or uneven ground, this should be shown up by a third transparency. Next, place the main skeletal features of the garden on the plan – paths, retaining walls and fences should all be marked in. Return to your initial plans and try to adapt them to what is physically possible.

The reverse approach of adapting the reality of the site to your desired design is usually possible, but will involve more time and often expense, and can produce trees and plants which will not yield such good results. The same disadvantage exists with ready-made plans. There is no shortage of these – they appear regularly in books and magazines – but they are designed for the 'average' garden. They cannot possibly take into account your plot size, the aspect, the micro-climate, or, more importantly, your likes and dislikes.

A similar criticism can be levelled at competition gardens and display gardens, where the primary aim is to impress the judges – the designer is not obliged to live with his creation. Such plans and designs are like ill-fitting clothes which have to be altered for the individual – the difference is that which exists between a ready-made suit and bespoke tailoring! Every gardener should try to live at peace with his garden, and must remember that Nature always seems to take back her own if we try to pervert it.

The features that you intend to create (as opposed to those which are already there) should be made as cut-outs. Decide the sizes relative to the size of the plot, and make the cut-outs larger or smaller accordingly. This is particularly important when you are considering ponds and rockeries. If your pond is too large, you will have a water garden with no room for other plants – any that are planted will give the impression of an afterthought that is not really part of the garden. A pond that is too small, on the other hand (as many are), will look like an outdoor sunken aquarium and be slightly ridiculous.

Height

Before you can finalise your plants you will need to consider the question of height in your garden. All too frequently gardens end up flat, uninteresting, and two-dimensional, and this is the result of not taking the planning process right through to the end. Even if a garden contains raised beds and sunken pools there is unlikely to be any deviation from the flat that is greater than 3ft (1m). Height gives to the garden the illusion of mass, and without some attempt to provide variation in height levels no garden can truly be described as being landscaped. Height must be created in a balanced form, the highest part in proportion to the rest of the plot. In the best landscaped schemes there will be a gradual, but not necessarily regular, rise in the height of the features from the front to the back of the field of vision. An alternative approach is a completely flat forefield with a background that rises sharply. This may be provided almost instantly by planting one of the quick-growing evergreens such as *Cupressocyparis leylandii*, or by the provision of buildings such as a wooden outhouse. The effect is further enhanced if a sunken pond is placed in front of the high feature. By far the best way to create height in a garden is to plant one of the slower-growing trees, although these will take a long time to achieve their full beauty. In the short term you could use one of the faster-growing forms but the slower-maturing subjects will always be more majestic.

Some slower trees you can choose from include willows which, when planted over water, seem to bestow their own form of peacefulness and tranquillity upon a scene, and acers with their delicate leaf shape which will provide harmonious colour throughout the summer. Birches, as well as giving form to a garden, provide interesting barks, and seem to prosper on most types of soil, both acid and chalk. They come in a variety of forms, including the silver

Fig 31 (facing page) A well-planned garden with border, lawn and paved area.

birch which is native to Britain (*Betula pendula*), the 10ft (3m) tall weeping birch which is a suitable subject for the smallest gardens (*B. pendula Youngii*), and the North American 'paper bark' birch (*B. papyrifera*).

Height should not be looked at solely in terms of the garden as a whole. Each bed should be considered both individually and in relation to the rest of the plot. This does not mean that some beds cannot be flat, and, indeed, in the formal-type setting many will be, but they should not all be of the same height. You will find that this is not difficult to achieve even where you are using summer bedding plants. The rule with all beds must be that the taller subjects are away from the eye, grading down to the smallest in the front and nearer to the observer. It is in the herbaceous border and mixed beds that the greatest care must be taken with positioning the subject according to its height, and due allowance must also be made for the size of the subjects when fully grown.

The same rules apply to each individual bed as to the garden as a whole – do not overcrowd, otherwise the beauty of all the subjects will be lost; no plant is at its best if it has to compete for space. One characteristic of a well-designed garden is that it is not possible to take everything in at one glance. The eye must be induced to scan the whole vista, assimilating the beauty of the garden bit by bit. Every view should present items of fresh interest to delight the eye. This is equally important in the vertical and the horizontal plane.

Colour

Colour is something that many gardeners tend to ignore. Together with shape, form and perfume, it makes up the four factors contributed by the plants, the most important subjects in the garden. Yet the vast majority of gardeners either omit it from their plans, or (worse) group together plants that clash and offend the eye. We would be unlikely to paper our walls with a pattern containing flowers of red, blue, green,

Fig 32 The use of colour. Subdued shades produce a softness throughout the beds.

violet, yellow and orange, all fighting to outshine each other, but that is exactly the effect that many people create in their gardens. The reason why so many gardeners fall into this trap is that they easily forget that the rules of colour co-ordination are just as important outside the house as inside, and they they apply to natural as well as to man-made decorations. Obviously, achieving harmony is easier with the latter as any colour you wish may be easily obtained. In the garden this problem is further compounded with the background of the sky – bright blue during the summer months, and so different in the winter. Winter skies are less difficult, and there are also far fewer brightly-coloured flowers in bloom at this time of the year – indeed, colour represents such a welcome diversion that we tend to accept with gratitude any that appears. With careful planning this, too, can be overcome. There is a surprisingly large number of plants that do flower and provide colour throughout the

winter months, as well as numerous twigs and branches (such as dogwood) that all contribute relief during the short dull days.

There is no reason to neglect a consideration of colour just because plants are natural. Nowhere in nature will you find so many different flowers growing in such close proximity as in a flower bed. The flowers may well bloom in our gardens in their natural seasons, but gardeners do bring together in one small plot plants from all over the world which would not normally co-exist. In the natural world there is no clash of colours. All plants must compete for resources, such as the services of insects, birds and other animals for fertilisation. The first plants to bloom naturally in the spring are the yellows – during late March and early April this colour takes over in both the garden and the countryside. It is believed that this is due to the pollinating insects that are flying at that time of year being attracted only to yellow. Whilst this is important to the survival of

Fig 33 The use of colour. The blue-green end of the spectrum adds up to perfect harmony.

the wild plant in its natural habitat, it is of no consequence to the imported garden species which do not depend upon the forces of natural selection. Other plants are bred and have no really close equivalents in the natural world — these are plants which have been produced by crossing two species, and sometimes these two species may even come from different continents. Nature itself does not create colours that . clash and you should try to do the same.

Colour Co-Ordination

To understand the principles of colour co-ordination you have to appreciate that there are three primary colours, and once you have these, other colours can be made up using combinations of them. In Fig 35 you can see that where two colours overlap a third colour is formed, and this is called a 'secondary colour'.

To create harmonising effects within a flower bed you may combine any primary colour with any secondary colour which contains that primary in its make-up. For example, red may be put with either orange or mauve, but not both in the same bed. As a general rule, you should not have two primary colours in the same scheme. Where all three colours come together, white is formed, and this blends perfectly with any colour. White creates the most harmonious of conditions and it is difficult to improve upon a scheme which makes use of white flowers and silver and white variegated foliage, but this, although restful, will be too restrictive for most gardeners. Bright colours need not be left out from the garden — instead, they should be used like jewels, with extreme moderation. For example, you could successfully plant a single group of daffodils amongst the whites and reds of a heather and conifer bed, or have an electric-blue gentian blooming in the rocks and sparse greenery of an alpine garden.

49

Fig 34 Summer is when most time is spent outside so a good show of colour around the patio area is essential. The creator of this garden has used a variety of brightly-coloured plants to excellent effect, making the most of many different types of container.

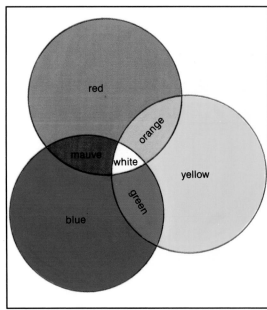

Fig 35 The colours of life. Colour harmonies are created with blends of red-orange-white, yellow-orange-white, red-mauve-white, blue-mauve-white, blue-green-white, and yellow-green-white.

Two colours that contrast, such as blue and yellow, may be used together in beds, but you must remember that the effect will be to draw attention to that particular bed in such a way that the eye of the observer will tend to disregard the surroundings. This technique is used in municipal landscaping, where the beds of a roundabout, for example, can draw the eye away from a backcloth of traffic and tarmac. Such schemes are designed to make an immediate impact on everyone who passes by, and there is no permanency about them – they are planted out for one season and once they have bloomed, they are destroyed. This represents a marked contrast with the work of the home gardener whose sole concern is to design a landscape that he can live with, and that will last for years, improving as it acquires maturity.

The Psychological Effect of Colour

Use can also be made of the psychological effect of colours to the benefit of the whole landscape.

Orange and red are 'warm' colours, while blues and greens are 'cold'. Warm colours will appear to shorten the distance between the subject and the observer, so that if you plant warm-coloured subjects to the front of the garden they will appear to be closer to you as you look at them. If you then create a garden of blue or green subjects at the farthest point, it will seem to be further away from the observer, giving the illusion of extra depth to the plot.

CREATING AN ILLUSION

It should be apparent that by using the principles of good landscaping you can easily create a desired illusion. A curved path leading towards green stately trees will do much to suggest that the urban garden is far larger than it really is, and such adjuncts to architecture are essential if we are to live within ever-smaller plots. Having decided upon the type of garden which you wish to make, and once you appreciate the rules

50

Fig 36 One way of treating a long narrow plot, with the path curving away into the distance.

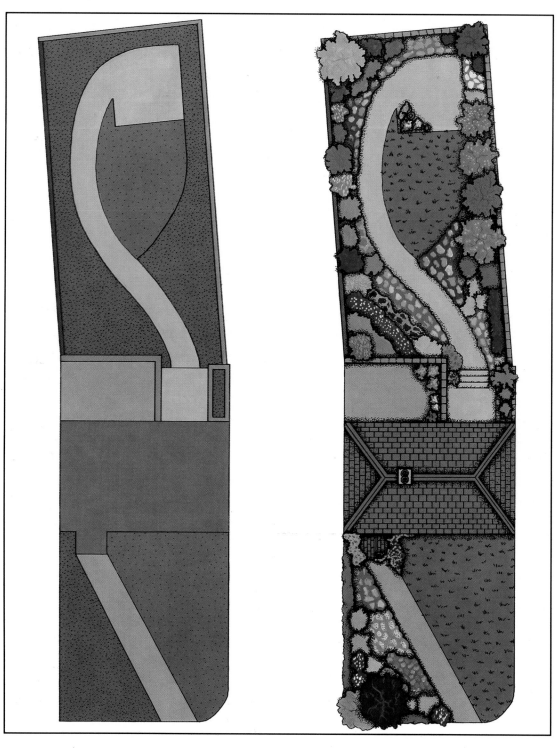

Fig 37 An alternative approach to an elongated property. The path has an important role, creating a focal point, and, with its curvature, appearing to increase the depth of the plot. Maintenance may be controlled by selecting the correct plants.

Fig 38 The overall harmony of the garden should become apparent as it matures and is something to consider at the planning stage.

governing the selection of plants for various positions you should realise that there are several different possibilities. When selecting your plants, try to ensure that there will be colour and interest in the garden throughout the year – if necessary, you can do this by marking out a plan showing how the garden will look in the different seasons. Before starting work, plan your earth movements. In virtually every landscaping operation it will be necessary to move earth, rocks and other materials. To reduce costs, establish whether any of the materials that you

already have can be re-utilised. If the answer is yes, then very careful consideration must be given to the movement of these materials. An extra set of movements can be avoided by carefully planning all stages of the operation.

There are no short-cuts in the planning process. Mistakes are more easily rectified and are far less expensive when they are committed in theory. By the end of this stage your landscape will have gradually evolved on paper, and it now remains to create it in your garden.

CHAPTER 4

Soil and Lawns

PREPARING THE SOIL

No landscaping scheme will succeed if the roots of perennial weeds are present in the soil. Simply digging the soil is not enough, as the roots will survive, and by chopping the roots of subjects such as couch grass you will only propagate the weeds. It is often recommended that you 'double-dig' virgin sites, but this process involves a great deal of time-consuming physical work, and is counter-productive unless the plot has a sufficient depth of top soil. A better approach is to dig the soil in the autumn and fork over in early spring (the earlier the better), and hand pick out the roots of the weeds. There will be hundreds of weed seeds in the soil – these are unavoidable, but present no problem if they are removed whilst they are still young. It is the creeping roots and rhizomes which spread into the crowns of other plants, and which are impossible to remove without taking out the cultivated plants. The other advantage of autumn digging is that, if the soil is left in a rough, unraked state, the compaction which has occurred on all land will be broken up by the action of expanding ice crystals. These will be formed during the frosts from the water in the soil. The result is that during the spring you will have a good tilth, a friable soil which will break down into small pieces when a rake is passed through it. Small soil-clump size is particularly important in the first year of any plant's growth, as, until such time as they are established, the conditions for them must be ideal, and that includes a good air supply to the roots and adequate drainage. Once the plants have become established they can survive a harsher environment, but care must still be

taken to ensure that plants other than pond or bog plants never have their roots permanently under water or they will die. Where soil preparation cannot commence until the spring, great care must be taken to break down the soil manually.

LEVEL

Depending upon the degree of slope, there are three possible ways of developing a sloping garden. Usually the least satisfactory answer is to leave it sloping: otherwise it may be levelled, which is time-consuming and involves much movement of soil, or it may be terraced.

To level a piece of sloping ground, take a piece of timber that is longer than the difference in the levels to be checked. Hammer it in at the lowest point of the garden. Hammer a shorter piece of timber 6ft (2m) up the slope into the ground until the top appears to be level with the top of the larger piece of timber. Place a plank across the top of the two pieces and adjust them with a hammer using a spirit level. Now take a second large piece of timber and hammer it into the ground beside the shorter piece and repeat the process. In this way you can make step-wise progressions up the plot, and you will end up with a series of level steps. If you wish these may be used as the basis for terracing. Alternatively you may mark out a straight guide string, from the top of the first pole. The string may be carefully checked for position with a hand-held spirit level, to ensure that it remains true.

Soil may now be moved from the high ground to the low ground. When moving soil, it is important that you remove the topsoil to a depth of about lft (30cm) and place it all to one side, and then level the soil underneath, before returning an even amount of topsoil to the area. If you do not adopt this technique you will have an area that is infertile, which will probably require the addition of large quantities of peat or other topsoil before it is capable of supporting worthwhile growth. Terracing is prepared by the same technique, only the levelling is done in a series of steps to create the escarpment. With either levelling or terrace construction you should check with a plank or a spirit level after the soil has been moved to its new position, to ensure that the area is truly flat.

THE HALLOWED LAWN

Few gardens will be successful without a lawn, and there are even fewer gardeners who would not wish to have one. Attempts to design a garden without a lawn should only be made after very careful consideration. This garden feature goes back to pre-Elizabethan times, although the first ones were probably herb lawns, planted with camomile – it was on such a surface that Drake probably played his famous game of bowls. Gravel may be used in place of lawns in very small areas, such as terracing or in front of a rockery, and paving stones may be laid in a patio with gaps for plants and troughs, and tubs for more plants. Both approaches can be used successfully, and may represent the most suitable method for civic landscaping where cost is the primary consideration. However, unless time restricts your approach to gardening the patio-type surface should be used on only one part of the garden and a lawn included to provide variety in the other.

Old Lawns

Unless you have just moved into a new property, you will in all probability have some sort of lawn. All or some of the area already under lawn may call for grass in your new scheme. Only after a thorough examination of the lawn already present should the existing grass be destroyed, as a new lawn will take a great deal of time to establish itself. Providing they are maintained, lawns do not age in the same way as plants. With a lawn there is continual regrowth, with new plants replacing the old ones, and as such there is no virtue in destroying and replanting a lawn solely because you believe that what is there has come to the end of its natural life.

Where a lawn is not cut regularly, the stronger, coarse, broad-leaved grasses, with a far more open growth pattern, are given the opportunity to take over from the faster-growing, fine-leaved plants, which will form the tight, compact lawn that you are seeking. Years of neglect and irregular cutting will result in a coarse, open-textured lawn, in which case replanting is the only satisfactory approach.

Lawns grow quickly and soon acquire a shabby look if they are not regularly cut – when you move into a property with an established garden, it may look overgrown as the result of just a fortnight's neglect. Also, when you start work on a garden you may be too busy to tend the lawn and it may suffer from being left alone even longer. This is unlikely to destroy the grass irreversibly, although you should attend to the lawn as soon as you start on the plot. Once you take up regular mowing the fast-growing grass cultivars (providing they are still present) will begin to gain the ascendancy over the coarse grasses, and very soon you will develop a quality lawn. If you are not confident of the width of the required grasses, examine some in a well-kept lawn. Cut your grass and examine it; stand back and see if the lawn is, or holds the potential to become, satisfactory. If in doubt, delay digging – instead cut the lawn again. There are only two seasons in which a new lawn may be planted – spring and autumn – so there is nothing to be gained by digging up the old lawn before you have had the opportunity to assess its ability to recover. Never judge a lawn in the autumn or winter as it will not be at its best, and will not

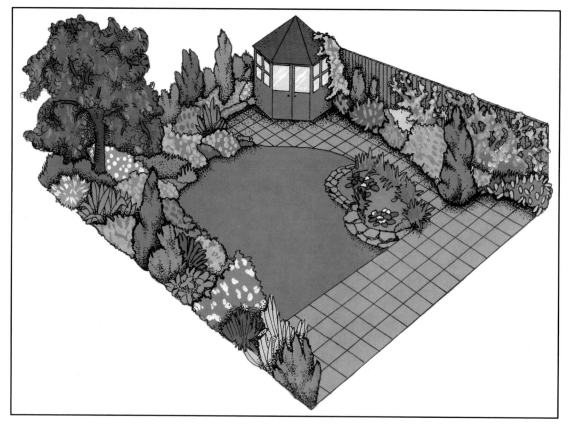

Fig 39 This is a garden for enjoying. Allowance is made for a specimen tree such as Betula (birch). A grass area is provided for colour. Note the bold curved path contrasting with the angular paving.

have the fresh look that you are seeking until it has been cut two or three times the following spring.

Restoring an Old Lawn

Even where a lawn is basically sound, there will often be parts that are worn or damaged in other ways. Where there is a worn patch away from the growing edge, fork over the damaged area during the sowing season, making sure that you go right up to the edge of the good lawn. Sieve the soil to ensure that it has a good tilth that is free from perennial weeds and stones, which would damage the mower. Where extra soil is needed to make up the level, sieve good

quality loam into the hole. Firm the soil down by walking over the surface, placing the heel of the one boot firmly in front of the toe of the other and giving an even press with the feet. When the piece has been firmly trampled down, check that it is level with the rest of the lawn. Sow with bird-repellant lawn seed at the rate of 2oz/sq yd (50g/sq m), or with non-treated seed at twice this rate. Cover the surface with cotton to stop birds and animals trespassing on to the newly-sown area.

Where the lawn has a worn patch at its edges, cut out as many turves as necessary, 24x24x2in (60x60x5cm), and reverse them so that the fresh, cut side is now in line with the edge of the lawn, and the worn portion is creating a depression in from the boundary of the lawn. This depression can then be treated by the same method given for worn patches. With small patches it is possible to effect the repairs and the sowing during the summer months, providing that portion of the lawn is watered daily and extra care is taken when it is cut.

Perennial weeds with a crown, such as dandelions and the several different varieties of plantain, are best treated with sulphate of ammonia. Sprinkle a small quantity on to the crown of the plant — this will kill it by osmosis, drawing the water out of the cells of the weed. It will also destroy a small area of the surrounding grass — how much will depend upon the quantity you use and how careful you are to ensure that it is spread only on to the weed. Do not be concerned about the patch of burnt grass and do not try to remove it. In spite of appearances, grass is more resistant to osmotic attack than the broad-leaved weeds, and will quickly recover. The ammonium sulphate will form nitrates in the soil that will actually stimulate growth so that for a short time after it has recovered, the grass may appear more lush where the weed has been destroyed. Sulphate of ammonia can be purchased far more cheaply than most proprietary weed killers, and if it is stored in a dry place it will keep indefinitely. If you have only a very small number of weeds, they can be killed with ordinary table salt, but this will have no fertiliser effect. Also, salt should not be used continually or on large quantities of weeds, as it is not desirable to have a build-up of large amounts of sodium chloride in the lawn.

Maintenance of the Lawn

Mowers and Mowing

The most important aspect of lawn maintenance is mowing. During the rapid growing season of late spring and early summer, your lawn should be cut twice a week, and this is another factor to bear in mind when designing the garden. If you cannot spend this amount of time on the garden,

a lawn may not be ideal and an alternative solution must be sought. Lawns will stand some neglect, and occasionally the cutting may be reduced to once a week. However, just prior to cutting the grass will lose its pristine look and, using most types of mower, it will take far longer to cut a neglected lawn than one that has been well looked after. Returning from a fortnight's holiday you will find that the grass is long but it will not be damaged, and will regain its former glory after just one cut.

Whether you use a hover or cylinder-type mower must remain a matter of personal choice. The old argument that the cylinder mower is better because it will give the much sought-after 'stripped' effect does not necessarily apply as it is now claimed that some rotary mowers will do just that. Before buying a mower, give very careful consideration to your needs. In a garden which has a large number of curves, for example, it is often impractical to produce a stripped effect. There may also be sunken stones for paths, and, while hover mowers can take a small amount of hard surface in their stride, if the fine-honed blades of the cylinder mower strike concrete, they will need to be resharpened. Of more importance is the method of propulsion. For very small areas you can use a hand-pushed cylinder mower, but for the majority of gardens the choice must lie between mains electricity, battery and petrol-driven. Whilst mains electricity is the most convenient, the cord can become cumbersome in all but the simplest of garden designs, and in a garden with curves and herbaceous beds you will find that it tends to get caught up in the bushes. There is also a limit to the distance that the mower can be used from a power point, and extension leads which can easily be fitted tend to aggravate the tangling problem. When using this type of mower always fit an automatic cut-out plug and take the greatest care not to cut the cord — unless you are careful this is all too easily done.

In spite of the disadvantages, mains supply mowers are the best for the small plots of the modern estate-type house but you must ensure that you do not buy an underpowered model. There are cheaper models that are designed for, and ideally suited to, the very smallest plots, but if they are used on modest-sized lawns that are inclined to be damp and are slightly long they will tend to over-heat and then cut out. If you are in any doubt, always buy the higher-rated model, but never buy a mower that is so large it cannot be comfortably manoeuvred around the garden.

If you have a large lawn your choice must be with battery- or petrol-driven models, and you will have to decide for yourself whether you prefer to collect petrol and have the bother of maintaining a small petrol engine, or recharge a battery. Neither of these tasks is particularly onerous. The mower is an important part of your equipment and needs maintenance itself, so you must have it sharpened and serviced once a year. This should be done during the winter months – there is always a rush when mowers are needed again in the spring, and you may find that you have to leave your machine in the shop for a week at a time when you need it. With care and attention your mower will give you many years' service, so choose it and look after it with care. Remember, without a good mower you will never have a good lawn.

The belief that you should not cut lawns during the winter months is incorrect. If it is allowed to remain uncut your grass will have a very untidy appearance which will be reflected throughout the garden. However, you should never cut the lawn when it is frosted or very wet. There *are* bright spells throughout the winter (except possibly in December), and the weather must dictate the frequency of cutting. Do not try to get on to the lawn simply because it has been a long time since it was last cut, but, rather, cut it whenever there is a dry spell. Remember that you cannot cut it too often. To avoid damage to the lawn set the mower at its highest – this should be done at any time of the year after a period has elapsed since the last cutting. In the summer months (but not the winter) where you have used the highest level, follow with a tighter cut to give a finer finish.

Aeration

Lawns tend to become compacted if you are continually walking on them, even if this is done only when mowing or carrying out general garden maintenance. In addition cut grass will lodge in the roots, particularly if the mower has no box to catch the cuttings. During the autumn you should scarify the surface with a long-toothed lawn rake. At every 12in (30cm) open the soil by inserting a fork to a depth of 2–3in (5–8cm), and moving it back and forwards slightly to allow the air to enter the roots. The more holes you make the more effective the aeration will be. Unless the air is allowed to get to the roots, the required fine grass cultivars are not going to survive, as compaction will favour the more resilient coarse-leaved forms. Lawns produce one of the largest growths in the garden in terms of the amount of cuttings that they produce each year. They are gross feeders which tend to deplete the soil of its minerals. One dressing of a good proprietary lawn fertiliser in the spring will serve to boost growth and maintain a good sward.

Moss

Occasionally lawns will suffer from the growth of moss, which will take over from the grass during the wet months and leave denuded patches in the summer. A brisk raking and treatment with a moss killer will solve the problem. Possessing only shallow roots grass is incapable of seeking water at great depths, and during periods of drought the lawn will become brown and barren. Unfortunately this is the time at which the rest of the garden will be looking its best. To retain the green colour it will be necessary to water daily during dry spells with a sprinkler. All watering is best carried out after sunset to allow the majority of the water to penetrate without evaporating off. Make sure that you check with your local water authority as many of them make an extra charge for the use of a sprinkler and hose.

Constructing a New Lawn

Where it is necessary to construct a new lawn you must decide whether you wish to use seed or turf. It is often said that a top quality lawn can only be made from turves, but this is not really correct. Turves are produced by seeding good quality loam and then lifting. Providing that you have a good quality topsoil there is no reason why you should not grow a top-of-the-range lawn by the far cheaper method of sowing. The only time that an amateur needs to consider using turves is when he does not possess the essential quality and depth of topsoil; he will certainly also find it more convenient to import topsoil than turves, unless he needs an instant lawn. You should remember, too, that if you use turves you will still need a good foundation, as they are unlikely to prosper if they are planted on to a poor surface. The use of turves is not a satisfactory way to overcome poor drainage either. If they are planted in a waterlogged site, even for only a small part of the year, they will simply rot.

Site Preparation

Where builders' rubble remains on a site, irrespective of your chosen method of creating the lawn, you should level the ground, remove all traces of the rubble and cover with imported topsoil.

With any site which is to be lawned the area must first be drained by laying pipes if there is any danger of waterlogging. Stones must be removed and the soil broken up by digging. At this stage the roots of any perennial weeds should be removed and any stones that surface must be taken away. The soil must be raked level – check with a plank and spirit level. Do not rely on your eye for this as there is nothing that can be done to remedy faults once the lawn has been laid. Finish by raking to a fine tilth. Buy seed which is covered in bird repellant, and if you are planning a hard-wearing lawn, which will serve for example as a children's play area, use a mixture containing rye grass. For a lawn of the highest quality you will require a mixture which does not include this coarse variety. To ensure an even distribution of seeds mark the area of lawn into lyd (lm) squares, place a piece of plank beside the square to stand on and sow the seed at the rate of 2oz/sq yd (50g/sq m). For an accurate measure, weight out 2oz (50g) into a can and mark the level on the side. You can then use the can for measuring out the portions for each square yard or metre. Make a protective meshwork of cotton – tie it about 2in (5cm) from the base of some pegs which should then be driven in around the border. When the seedlings are 2.5in (6cm) tall the grass should be cut. This is the most important cutting of the lawn – choose a day when the soil is firm, do not wear heavy boots and place the mower at its highest setting. Carelessness at this stage can result in the unsecured seedlings being torn out by their roots.

If you are planning to lay out turves, an accurate base line must be constructed, relative to the house wall, or other point of reference on the plan. The first row of turves should be laid to form a straight edge against the base string. Cut a turf in two and with one of the halves start the second row. The half turf is then followed by a full turf to give a staggered effect – this will add necessary extra strength to the bonding of the turves. When laying turves always use a plank as a duck board, to avoid uneven compression of the soil. Turves are living systems but they are not immediately part of the garden system and until the roots have penetrated the subsoil the grass will be incapable of drawing up its own water. They must be watered regularly until they are established or else they will die – in that case, you will have bought for yourself some very expensive topsoil.

Marking out Areas

When sowing seed, much of the marking out of the garden design can be accomplished on the soil before it is seeded and the seed is then sown right up to the edges of the boundaries of the beds. With turves it is far more satisfactory to plant in straight lines relative to a reference point, then you can cut out the various shapes *after* the lawn is well established. Sown lawns can also be left until they are established, and the principle of cutting remains the same. Grass is best marked out and then cut with a spade, before being finished with an edging tool which is a spade in the shape of a half-moon.

ESTABLISHING FOCAL POINTS

To find the true centre of a plot, garden, or lawn within a garden take four pegs and place one at each of the corners. Attach strings diagonally and measure the length of the diagonal, then cut a piece of string one-third of this length. Tie the shorter piece of string to a peg inserted in the centre of the plot, where the first strings cross, and allow it to run alongside the first pieces of string in four directions. The end of the second piece of string in each case will give you the focal points (marked A, B, C and D in Fig 40) as seen from both ends of the lawn or garden. With the house situated in the corner (*see* Fig 40) the true boundary of the garden rather than that of the garden minus the house or outbuilding should be obtained. This presents no problem, providing

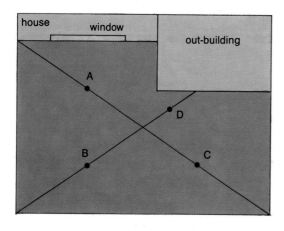

Fig 40 Finding the focal points of the garden.

Fig 41 Here an eye-catching show of clematis 'Montana Rubens' is displayed to spectacular effect on a brick well in the lawn area to provide an interesting focal point.

that the reference point D can be pegged out in line with the true corner. In this example, B will be the focal point to which the eye will be most naturally drawn. The area between the house and A may be partitioned off with a trellis, a hedge or espalier fruit trees. The area around C can be out of site, creating an area of mystery, if it is partitioned off by a trellis work or a pergola. This effectively creates a false boundary and you should now redefine your focal points with reference to the structure rather than to the true boundary of the garden. In landscaping terms it is often impossible to distinguish between the whole area to be landscaped and just the lawn where the former contains a very large area of grass.

Marking Out a Circle

For this you will need one sharp wooden or metal peg, a length of string and a second peg which is driven into the ground at the centre of where you want the circle to be. Attach the

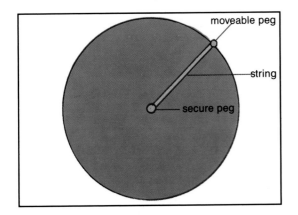

Fig 42 Marking out a circle.

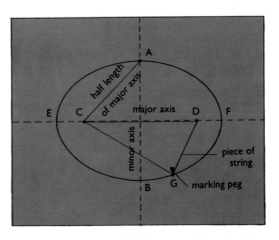

Fig 43 Marking out an oval shape.

string to the centre peg and at one half of the required diameter of the circle tie the sharp peg to the string. Hold the string taut and mark the circle with the peg (see Fig 42). Where a circular bed or circle is to be cut around a tree trunk, the trunk itself may be allowed to serve as the central pivot, providing that care is taken not to damage the bark.

Marking Out an Oval

Whereas all points on the circumference of a circle are the same distance from the centre, an oval has a major and a minor axis and allowance must be made for this when marking out. Find your required centre point. Then mark, by means of powdered chalk or indentation, a cross with the lines at right-angles to each other. Mark the position so that you know approximately the greatest distance from the centre in all directions. Then ensure that the distances either side of the centre are the same, so that you now have a cross with the two sides of different length, a longer and a shorter — these will be the major and minor axes respectively. It does not matter what the ratio of the two lengths are to each other — basically the greater the difference the less the curvature.

The oval will have two centres of curvature. To find these, place a peg at point A and with a piece of string half of the length of the major axis,

mark an arc which cuts the major axis at two points, C and D. Firmly fix two pegs at points C and D to act as anchor points. A piece of string is measured out at twice the length from D to E, the position where the circumference cuts the major arc at its greatest distance from D. This is made into a loop. (Note: When measuring out the piece of string due allowance must be made for the knot, as it is the internal measurement that must be equivalent to DE.) The loop is hooked over pegs D and C, and a sharp pointed peg is placed inside the loop at G. This peg is then moved towards B, marking out the shape in the process. Whilst still in the string triangle it is moved towards E. The procedure is then repeated on the other side of AF, so that it travels through A and F and back to G.

This principle, together with that described for marking out a circle, will form a basis of marking out all curved edges. Where a curve other than a circle is required, it should be seen as part of an oval — it could, for example, correspond to the curve EAF in Fig 43. To construct it you must again define your major and minor axis and, providing you have sufficient room, you can treat it as for the total oval but only cut out the marked part which you require.

For a scalloped effect each of the 'shells' will be either an arc of a circle or a complete semi-circle.

61

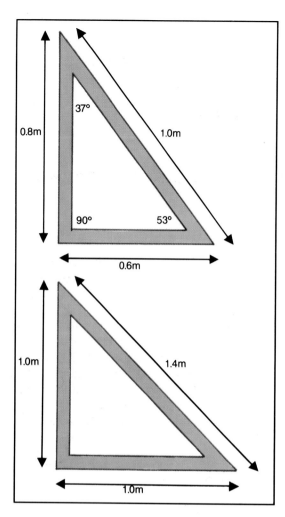

Fig 44 Making a suitable set square. This will allow you to set the correct angles for beds. As an alternative, an isosceles with 45 degree angles may be made.

Fig 45 Curves can be incorporated into the shape of the lawn to create an informal layout as above. Note also the use of the gas lamp which serves as an interesting focal point.

For the best results, use the latter, in which the width is twice the depth. To achieve this, place a string base line at a distance of half the radius from, say, the edge of an existing lawn. Then, using a peg and a piece of string, mark out an arc on the area to be delineated. Move the base string along the distance of the diameter of the circle and repeat the process. Continue until the scalloping effect is complete.

More elaborate shapes are sometimes desirable for the centre-piece of certain garden features, and one of the most popular is a cluster of circles. Decide how big you want the circles to be then mark out a square whose centre lies at the centre of the feature, and whose sides are equal to the diameter of the circles. Use each of the corners of the square as the centre of a circle, and draw the circles. The resultant lines outside the square will make up the boundary of the required shape. With an elongated garden you may follow the general pattern and create an elongated cluster by using a diamond.

All sorts of shapes can be built from angles and circles, but the whole effect will be spoilt if you do not work from the true centre, have accurate angles and symmetrical curves. If it is absolutely impossible, due to access or other reasons, to mark out accurately, then you must rely on your eye. Mark out areas with powdered lime, chalk dust or even talcum powder, to give you a line which you can easily erase, and make adjustments to it before marking out the firm base line from which you will work. If you do have to rely solely on your eye, it is imperative that the markings are studied from all possible angles before any turf is actually cut.

CHAPTER 5

Ponds and Water Gardens

PONDS

Depending upon its mood, water can be the most passive or dynamic of all the elements, and both these characteristics can be used to good effect in the garden. Still water, say, in the form of a pond covered in blooming water-lilies, gives the impression of peace and tranquility, and this effect can be created only feet away from a busy main road. If you add a small electric pump to move the water around or to create a fountain, the whole garden will seem to be alive.

The idea that you cannot create a garden without a pond is something of an exaggeration, but very careful consideration should be given to including a pond in even the most modestly-sized gardens. A pond is unique amongst garden features in that it has its own enclosed eco-system, with fish darting between the water-lilies, their bright colours as attractive as any in the garden. During the spring you may find frog- or toad-spawn as these amphibians push further and further into urban areas. So, if you are seeking to make your garden a wildlife haven, nothing will do this more effectively than the provision of a pond. Bees and butterflies will stop to drink and the increased insect life in the vicinity of the water will attract a wide range of birds, as well as newts and other creatures that are so much a feature of our fast-diminishing countryside.

Ponds may be either large or small; they may be the centre-piece or main feature, or they may be the secret which lies just around the corner

from the shrub bed, out of sight of the house. This will probably be the best place for the aspiring garden naturalist to site his water, whereas other designs should be out in the open, aiming to create the maximum visual impact, yet at the same time remaining unobtrusive. They can be included as part of a Mediterranean-type patio, or they may contribute to all of the garden, so that the water system is virtually the only item, with all other items serving only to support and emphasise the garden. The variations on the use of water are endless.

Pond Construction

Fibre Glass Moulds

Gone are the days of the old concrete ponds. Correctly constructed, a concrete pond is without peer and if you move into a house that already has one, unless it completely spoils your design you would be well advised to adjust your plans to fit in around it. It is likely to give you years of trouble-free service, and even where slight cracks do appear it is possible to buy a sealant to repair them. However, if it is not correctly constructed (and it is neither easy nor cheap to make a concrete pond), it will crack very easily and will be far more trouble than it is worth. If you are planning to build a pond then the simplest modern method of all is to use a fibreglass liner. These can be obtained in a variety of shapes and sizes and they usually have a step-like appearance, with the shelf providing the

facility for the growing of marginal plants. These are subjects which grow with their roots and lower stems covered with water. It *is* possible to create an effective water garden without providing for the growth of marginals but it is inadvisable for where the pond is going to occupy a significant part of the garden, the marginals, as well as being interesting subjects in their own right, provide a smooth gradation from the water to the terrestrial garden. In this way you avoid producing the hard contrast of water, stone or (worse) concrete alongside grass which is so often seen.

Once you have decided on the position of your pond, you can dig out the site to allow for the shape of your pond mould. Make sure that there are no stones, especially sharp flints – once the mould has been pierced it is very awkward to repair it. Before placing the mould in the hole cover the bottom of the excavated area with a layer of damp sand, old carpet or sacking material. Lower the mould into the hole, and when it is in position ensure that it is level by placing a plank across the top and checking with a spirit level. It is important with all ponds to ensure that they are absolutely level, otherwise when the water comes to rest, it will appear to be at different depths on opposing sides. With fibreglass moulds it is necessary to ensure a level surface and a firm foundation, otherwise the weight of water, which will be quite considerable, will be unevenly distributed. This will cause stress which could weaken and possibly damage the mould. When you are satisfied, pack damp sand between the mould and the contours of the hole.

Pool Liners

Pool liners can be used to make ponds of a greater size and more complicated shape than those that are possible with fibreglass moulds. Pool liners are sheets of waterproof plastic, which are laid into a hole in the ground and, as they become filled with water, they take on the shape of the hole. The pressure of the water on the soil walls creates the pond, with the liner serving as a waterproof membrane to stabilise the system. To decide the dimensions of liner you will need, allow the width (or length) of the pool, plus twice the depth together with 30in (79cm) to allow for an overlap of 15in (38cm) on all sides of the pool.

There are various types of plastic liners, covering a wide range of man-made chemical materials. Some are vulnerable to the ageing process as a result of frosts. Avoid cheap polythene liners, and choose the more expensive polyvinyl chloride (PVC or butyl rubber). Having bought your liner excavate the pond, again checking that there are no stones that could damage the very thin sheeting. Lay the sheet into the hole, which should be lined with damp sand or peat, and temporarily secure the overlap with either planks or large pieces of rockery stone. Do not attempt to fix it at this stage. Lay the hose in the lined hole and turn on the water supply. The liner will form a bag and begin to take the shape of the excavated pool. If any part of the plastic appears to be under strain release the hold on the overlap; it is better to do this even if you are using one of the stretch liners, for, although they possess more elasticity, unnecessary stretching can cause stress and should be avoided. Fill to within 2in (5cm) of the top of the hole. Fix the sheet permanently in position by covering the overlap with paving slabs, crazy paving, bricks or whatever material your plan demands.

Where fish are to be kept (and you are going to lose an important dimension to your water gardening if they are not) it is necessary to provide a sheltered area out of direct sunlight, where they can spend most of the day basking. The simplest way of achieving this it to allow a 4in (10cm) overlap of the paving slabs, but visually it is far better to construct a bridge or other piece of garden architecture.

Fig 46 (facing page) The fully formal pond has a special majesty all its own.

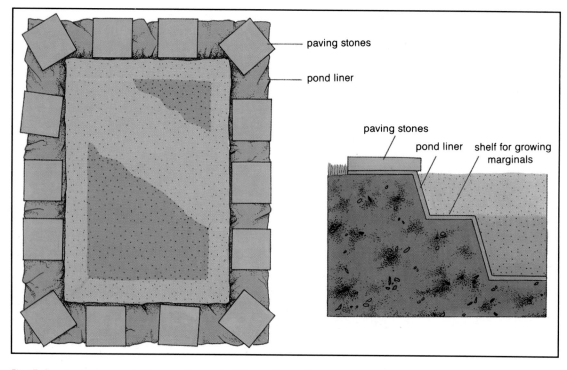

Fig 47 Constructing a pond. The pond liner is held in position with stones around the edge and the water forces the liner to take up the shape of the pond.

Bridge Building

The idea of bridge building in a small garden may seem very ambitious, but few features can create the impression of a sculptured garden better. A bridge will give a simultaneous sense of permanency and a feeling of empathy between the man-made structures and the creations of nature. A brick-built bridge will last a lifetime, but its construction requires a great deal of skill, and unless you are very proficient with a trowel you will need to employ a bricklayer. Only if you have a very large water garden will you need to have a brick-built structure that will be walked on constantly, but the full visual effect can be created using a wooden structure, cut and shaped plywood, with the sides as ornate as you wish. Where a bridge is not fully load-bearing it may be painted and maintained by working from planks laid across the pond. Unless you intend to create

a Japanese-style garden do not be tempted to paint your bridge in vivid colours – the rules of harmony still apply, and even the subdued bridge will be immediately spotted by the most casual of observers.

Stepping-Stones

For purposes of access, and for visual beauty, stepping-stones of the same rock formation as is used for the side of the pond are ideal. They are especially suited where a natural rock landscape is created to form part of a mountain side, covered in alpines, that appears to drain into the pond, complete with its marginals. What you are doing here in fact is attempting to recreate in miniature a favourite type of landscape, combining the two natural elements of stone and water, with the stepping-stones an integral part of that scenario. Such an effect, which can be

Fig 48 An example of a modern approach to water gardening. Although water is the main feature of any pond, here its role is secondary to that of the bridge which allows scope for creative woodwork. A rustic bridge would be more appropriate in some gardens.

captured in even the most modestly-sized garden, is not beyond the scope of any gardener, and may be achieved over a period of time. Various elements can be completed over ensuing years, but you must remember that you can only build by instalments if your final plan is done before any work is started on the site.

Where stepping-stones are being planned, or the use of water is being considered, thought must be given to the question of *safety*. It is possible to drown in less than 1⅓in (3cm) of water, and children should never be allowed to play near ponds. The safest thing is not to create a pond where children are likely to play.

Siting

Design-wise the siting of the pond is very important. A pond may be placed anywhere in the garden, but it is a virtual waste of this type of feature if it is thought of simply as a space filler. All too often ponds are hidden away as though the designer is apologising for their very existence. Although most ponds are flat, the eye of the observer will always wander towards them, and in planning their position you should think in terms of your preferred view from the main window and the focal points. A pond makes an excellent principal focus for any garden.

67

Fig 49 A two-level pond constructed from liners and surrounded by local sandstone. For ponds or rock gardens, always try to use the stone of the locality as this will create a far less artificial appearance.

In all but the most formal layouts, the best position is under a tree, and if your garden has any depth at all the best tree is the weeping willow (Salix chrysocoma). A pendulous willow hovering over water creates the idyllic pastoral scene of England during the lazy hazy days of summer better than any other characteristic. Smaller gardens will not be able to carry the relative size of the native willow. Again, remember that the best approach to landscaping such sites is to try and do everything in proportion, so seek out dwarf weeping willows, or any other tree with a weeping growth for which you have a preference, and place this over

the pond. A strategically-sited tree can also provide the necessary cover for fishes without recourse to other forms of shading, should you wish. Trees have a disadvantage as far as ponds are concerned, in that they shed leaves, but do not be tempted to solve the problem by planting a conifer. Not only are conifers not as visually acceptable as the broad-leaved trees in this location, but they also shed their leaves and tend to do so all the year round, unlike the deciduous varieties which restrict this activity to the autumn. Conifers also provide virtually no shade. For the six short weeks of autumn it is important that you place a net over the surface of the water

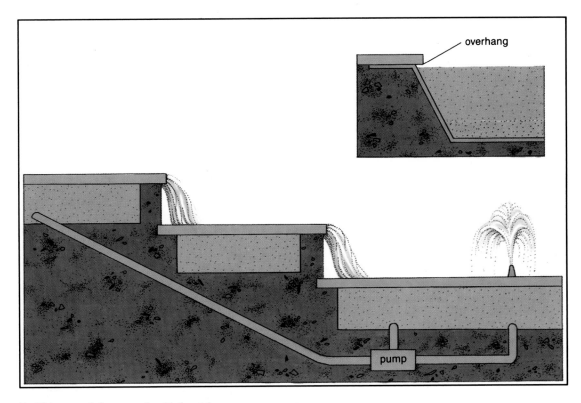

Fig 50 Layout of three ponds with fountain.

to catch the leaves. If the leaves are allowed to fall into the water they will begin to decompose, and this decomposition will use up most of the available oxygen in the water. It is this oxygen that the fish breathe and if it is not available to them they will die and the pond will become stagnant.

Movement

The use of a small electric pump will allow you to create movement of water in the garden. As a design feature this is unique and it is the only way to give a garden any vitality. Gardens are static, and, whilst they are always altering, the rate of change is so slow as to be imperceptible to the human eye, so the only form of natural movement within a garden is that of birds or butterflies. Both of these are dependent upon the season of the year, the ambient temperature

and the time of day, and often when we do have the chance to stop and pause to enjoy the garden it is too late in the evening. If you want your garden to come alive you can import the gentle but vibrant movement of water. Where it is thought desirable artificially to create visual interest in this way, the siting of the water becomes more important. Where movement is to be introduced the water should be sited at the principal focus of the design as it will be the sole dynamic feature of the garden.

Movement can be produced in two ways — either by means of a waterfall which involves two, or sometimes three levels, with the water being pumped up to the higher level and then allowed to cascade over rock surfaces down to a collecting pool before being recycled; a more dramatic effect can be created by the use of a fountain, again with a pump providing the necessary pressure. It is possible to achieve both

69

effects using one pump by incorporating an off-take before the pumped water rises to create the jet effect of the fountain. The rate of pumping will depend upon the capacity of the pump. As with most electrical equipment it is important not to try to economise and buy a pump of lower rating than is really necessary. There are two types of pump available, the submersible, which as the name implies lies in the pond, and the surface pump. Apart from the disadvantage that a suitable housing must be provided for it with a water inlet and outlet nozzle, the surface pump is less expensive and more versatile. The pump itself must be situated by the side of the pond and the garden designer should create something to hide the hideous man-made monstrosity which will spoil the effect. It is best housed in a box, opening away from the observer, and camouflaged with the use of rocks and strategical planting.

The tubing, again hidden, should lead up the escarpment to the highest of a set of fibreglass trays, which blend into the background. Each one will fill with water then overflow at the lip into the tray below (if you intend using more than one level) or the pond, to finish the water cycle. It is possible to make the trays yourself using a simple mould and a mixture of 4 parts concrete, I part sand and I part peat. Ensure that you form a good lip whilst the mixture is still wet. The trays should be placed at about 10in (25cm) intervals, one above the other, and secured with stones, the joints being filled with loam as if you were making a rockery. Under the prevailing damp conditions moss will soon grow and the whole structure will take on a more natural effect.

There are fibreglass creations that are a variation on the theme of a waterfall, the water passing not into trays but inside, say, pitchers, giving the impression that they never empty. The use of statues and models around or in a pond depends very much upon how well they are made. Those which tend to imitate works of art will help to achieve the impression of a gothic-type garden landscape of the classical school and can be very effective, but they should not be used in isolation. Such landscape gardening depends upon massive parklands to show off the full beauty of the sculpture; again it *can* be created in miniature, with the fibreglass statues being scaled down, and it will work providing that you have a sufficiently large garden to create a parkland-type background. Such figures are at home with rhododendrons, azaleas and magnolias, but when used in conjunction with the patio-type approach are totally out of place, often appearing as yet another man-made artefact used to replace plants and trees. Other concrete or plastic figures, such as a stork fishing, can, if they are of a size and natural-looking, add interest. However it is a *very* thin line that separates the pleasing from the absurd when it comes to garden statues. Whilst the question of taste is always subjective many people would agree that garden gnomes are faintly ridiculous and represent one of our most absurd fashions in urban gardens. Think carefully before purchasing any of these models not just for siting around the pond, but anywhere in the garden.

In a small garden it is important that the use of water should not be over-done. It should be a part of the whole, with architectural harmony being as important as the selection of mutually-compatible colours.

Lighting Near the Pond

When the still, warm evenings are beginning to draw in, the garden can be at its most pleasant for an *al fresco* meal or a quiet drink, with the flowers emitting the maximum amount of perfume to attract the night-flying insects (mainly moths, that do so much of the pollinating at this time of the year). The shortening of the days means that there is far less to see in the garden, but this problem can be overcome by fitting lights to the electrical supply laid on for the pond. Two lights, strategically placed on either side of a pond and concealed by bushes so that they are not seen during the day-time, can be switched on in the evening to create an entirely different vista. In siting the lights do not restrict the illuminated

Fig 51 A rock garden and pond combined give a pleasing contrast of heights, colours and textures creating a natural look in this area of the garden. Marginals and bog plants complete the overall appearance.

area to the water garden, but move them round to the flower beds and find the best position or positions on which to focus the lights. Gardens bathed in artificial light take on a completely different, almost mystical, appearance. If evening is the only time that you can spend enjoying your garden during autumn, use lights, and when planning the position of the beds and, more importantly, what they contain, design the area with the use of illuminations in mind.

Always use a qualified electrician.

WATER GARDENING

A pond with clear water through which you can see fish, and with water-lilies whose vivid colours are strong enough to be the 'jewel' of that particular part of the garden is a thing of beauty, requiring only the minimum amount of maintenance. However, it cannot be achieved without a little care and attention to detail. Were the pond to be filled simply with water, fish and water-lilies, the fish would soon die and the water would become a thick soup of micro-organisms, that would not clear of its own accord. The pond is an ideal growing medium and if you don't plant it then nature will, initially through air-borne microbes. These micro-organisms are anaerobes, or living things which prosper where there is little or no oxygen. Oxygen is essential to all higher forms of life but effectively poisons many microbes. Like all green plants, water-weed generates oxygen, most of which will dissolve in the water, simultaneously destroying the microscopic growths and aerating

71

the water to enable the fish to breathe. In addition all plants require minerals, and the stronger-growing water weeds and minerals will take those that are available at the expense of the microbes, further ensuring that the environment is hostile to the pond's enemies.

In spite of their total adaptation to an aqueous environment, water weeds and lilies require soil to provide minerals and anchorage for their roots. Purpose-built baskets can be bought for water-lilies to hold them at the bottom of the pond, and for water weeds you can make a suitable holder from the bottom of a washing-up liquid container. Cut several holes in the vessel to allow the roots free ventilation, and include a small quantity of lead in the container to ensure that it remains anchored. This small amount of lead will not harm the fish – at one time the best ponds were made out of this heavy metal. The temptation is always to plant too many water lilies, but where a small pond is constructed amongst rocks one bright colour will suffice. A large pond may take on the role of a true water garden, and you may plant more than one variety, but do allow at least 1sq yd (1sq m) for each plant. This will give total coverage in three to four seasons. To maintain vigorous growth it is necessary to lift the roots when there is total coverage, and divide the rhizome in two with a very sharp knife. Replace the soil in the container with fresh loam – lilies require large quantities of nitrogen to support the very large growth – and replant with a piece of the lily rootstock. Do not destroy your excess water-lily cuttings, as they are not easy to obtain and unlike most garden surplus can be readily sold to horticultural suppliers looking for stock, or disposed of through shop window advertisements.

Once established, ponds require very little work and the plants themselves, apart from the necessity of periodical thinning out, are problem-free. Fish, however make an attractive meal for next door's cat and, should you live near to a river, the odd heron may come and take one. If either of these predators present a problem you will need to cover the pond with a nylon mesh.

It is imperative that you place the mesh in such a way that it is anchored down, and yet not readily seen – even a green net will detract from the natural appearance which can be created. The other danger to the fish is ice – they need an ice-free area in order that the oxygen of the air can dissolve in the water. During the winter months keep a ball in the pond, as this will tend to move about and stop the pond from freezing over completely. It will not stop ice forming on the very coldest mornings. The fish will almost certainly have survived the night, but it will be necessary to provide an ice-free area as soon as possible and this should be achieved by pouring hot water on to the ice to melt it. Under no circumstances should you attempt to break the ice physically, as this will cause vibrations to form in the water and the shock waves created will kill the fish.

Marginals and Bog Plants

The difference between a marginal and a bog plant is one of degree: the roots and lower stems of marginals are under water, whereas bog plants require a saturated soil. Nature does not provide the clear-cut demarcations that man seeks, and several of the plants are capable of surviving in either environment, but it is wrong to think that such plants are not particular in their require-ments and the wetlands conditions must be maintained even during times of drought. Neither should these plants be considered as a simple alternative to draining a soil, as undrained soils do not have the constant water level required, and are often only wetlands during the winter months. Natural ponds lie in low ground, with the soil getting progressively wetter until it lies below the water table. The sides of the pond are not definite and they will change with the seasons. This has led to a gradation of plants adapted to the whole spectrum of different water levels. With larger gardens a similar approach to this is possible, but there is insuf-ficient space in the small modern garden, and the problem is overcome in the construction of the pond. The moulded pond has its shelf for marginals, but you can produce a far better gradation of depth by using a pond liner and creating a slope on one or two sides so that you may grow both marginals and bog plants.

Flag lilies (bearded irises) can be grown in most gardens but they look far more natural when grown as a marginal – in nature their ancestors are often found at the water's edge. Rushes (bulrushes, with their extra bonus for the flower arrangers) all tend to produce a natural and smooth gradation from land to water. Because of their height they should be sited to the side of the water garden, otherwise they will obliterate the view of the pond from the house, and the visual amenity will be destroyed. Primulas are a large family of over a thousand varieties that we are all familiar with as house plants, but many of

them will grow near water, and two or more species grown together will often hybridise and the self-set plants will emerge in a range of colours. The primula family, also found in alpine environments with their dainty compact form, offers one of the finest opportunities to anyone who wishes to create a plant collection. Other groups which represent a chance to collect plants which grow near water are the *ranunculus*, with its globular flowers, of which the common meadow plant, the buttercup, is a member, or the similar-looking *trollius*. The combined effect of damp and shade also creates the ideal environment for one of the oldest and most curious families of the plant kingdom, the ferns. These date from before the time when plants had developed the art of seed formation and rely

Fig 52 The formal pond can be enhanced with plants and ornaments.

Fig 53 A waterfall gives a sense of sound and movement to the garden. This one in natural stone has several levels and is planted round about with water-loving plants.

Plants for Ponds and Wetlands

Bog Arum	*Calla palustris*	White; arum lily-type flowers
Bulrush	*Scirpus tabernaemontani* sp	A backcloth to a pond which has both mass and form
Iris	*Iris kaempferi*	May–June; a range of colours including blue, white and yellow
Japanese Arrowhead	*Sagittaria sagittifolia*	White flowers; leaves the shape of arrow heads
Marsh Marigold	*Caltha palustris*	Yellow; one of the earliest to flower
Miniature Water-lily	*Nymphaea* 'Pygmaea Helvola'	Yellow; 6–12in (15–30cm) of water; variegated leaves; probably the best cultivar for patio ponds
Reed Mace	*Typha minima*	Useful in small gardens; has appearance of miniature bulrush
Spearwort	*Ranunculus lingua*	Buttercup-like flowers typical of the family
Water-lily	*Nymphaea* 'Escarboucle'	Ruby-red; 12–24in (30–60cm) of water; one of the longest-lasting varieties
Water-lily	*Nymphaea* 'James Brydon'	Carmine; 12–24in (30–60cm) water; double flowers

on spores formed under their fronds for propagation. These spores may be purchased from seedsmen and germinated in a similar manner to seeds.

For the designer who is seeking to create a natural area in the garden, the water and wetland garden has a great deal to offer. In addition the maintenance time is minimal, as there is very little danger of 'weeds' occurring in the water. These gardens need far less time than, for example, lawns, and the only regular attention that is required is that of feeding the fish.

Fig 54 The informal pond with marginal plants. The heron adds a point of extra interest.

CHAPTER 6

Vegetables, Fruit and Herbs

THE VEGETABLE GARDEN

There are some vegetables that can only be enjoyed to the full if they are eaten on the same day that they are harvested. No method of preservation or rapid transport from the farmyard to the shop can retain the delicate flavours or the crispness that are the hallmark of freshness. If you are to enjoy these vegetables then you have no alternative but to grow them yourself, and there is no reason why the modern garden should not incorporate a vegetable plot. Such an area will of necessity be far smaller than in former years, but we no longer need to grow potatoes, onions and the root crops which were once the mainstay of the diet, and which were grown at home for purely economical reasons. Should you wish to grow these vegetables then you are better off renting an allotment from the local council. When you consider the cost of a house and garden it is poor economics to use most of the space for vegetable cultivation at the expense of landscaping, when a large growing area can be rented for what is by comparison little more than a nominal sum.

The reduction in size of the modern vegetable plot does not mean that we cannot make worthwhile contributions to the kitchen, nor that the area in which they are growing need be ugly. Modern views on vegetable production have led to a rethink on the way that we actually grow them, and we know now that is it not necessary to have a large space between plants. Providing that there is *adequate* room, there is no

advantage in the generous gaps between the rows which were once thought essential if large crops were to be harvested.

Siting

Where room allows, the vegetable garden should be sited where it can receive direct sunlight, but not as part of the focus from the main window of the house. It may form part of a secret garden, or it may be separated from the rest of the garden by two protruding flower beds which leave only a small visual gap. Perhaps one of the best ways of screening off a vegetable plot is to use espalier apple trees.

Vegetable gardens need not be ugly – many are things of beauty in their own right. It is no longer important, for example, to grow vegetables regimented in rows; rather, you can easily allow them to be set out in blocks. Runner beans can be grown at the back of a garden (where their shadows cannot have an adverse effect on other subjects), and can be trained up around a teepee structure. The height of this will perform a similar role in terms of landscaping to that of a tree.

Rather than having just one large area for the vegetable plot, subdivide it, by means of paths, into small pieces in which you can work. Much of the area of a large vegetable plot is taken up with the space between the rows, and neat pathways will do much to take away some of the starkness. Many gardeners see this as their 'crop area', where sweet peas, dahlias and other varieties of cut flowers are grown alongside the vegetables to provide decoration for the house. This sort of approach is bound to make the area appear more attractive, as will growing the vegetables in blocks in the French style.

Soil

In this area of intensive horticulture the soil must be kept in tip-top condition, and this means that a regular supply of manure or compost will need to be worked into the ground. Well-rotted farmyard manure, spent mushroom compost or garden compost should be dug in every three years. The year before the ground is due for manuring it should be given a light sprinkling of lime – unlike the majority of flowers that do not like lime, virtually all vegetables either benefit from an occasional dressing of it, or at least are not harmed by it. The lime will also react with the almost spent manure to release the last vestiges of nitrogen to the plants, effectively gaining another year's life out of the fertiliser.

Protection

The modern vegetable garden needs to produce far more than its predecessor per square metre, and this can be greatly helped if glass or plastic is used. Cloches, cold frames and greenhouses will all yield crops long before they have reached the shops, as well as such delicacies as cantaloupe melons that are seldom available.

Vegetables

Asparagus

Prepare a well-drained bed the previous autumn by working in well-rotted manure or compost. The plants may be grown from seed, but that way they will take at least three years before a crop is raised. It is far better to purchase one-year-old plants, and modern varieties will allow you to take a small crop in the second year. Plant the crowns 24in (60cm) apart in rows that are 24in (60cm) apart themselves. In the autumn you must cut back the foliage (which is ideal for floral decoration) to just above ground level, and then mulch with well-rotted manure or compost. In the spring spread 2½oz/sq yd (70g/sq m) of Growmore fertiliser. Harvest the asparagus by cutting the shoots when they are 6–8in (15–20cm) high, to 1in (2.5cm) below the surface.

Beans – Dwarf or French

Prepare a trench 10in (25cm) wide by 10in (25cm) deep. Line the trench with newspaper followed by 2in (5cm) of well-rotted manure. Fill to the surface level with the excavated soil. The beans should be raised individually in pots and started in the greenhouse or conservatory from the second week in May for planting straight out into the prepared ground. Plant two rows, one at each edge of the trench, with the individual beans 6in (15cm) apart. For an earlier crop plant three weeks sooner and cover with cloches. Successive sowings may be conducted until the middle of July, and with these you may plant the seeds straight into the trench. If it has not completed its cropping before the onset of the first frosts, the last sowing should be protected by the cloches. It is important that the beans (which are ready for harvesting 8–10 weeks after planting) are cropped when they are the size of a pencil, to ensure that they are not tough and that the maximum crop is obtained.

Beans – Runner

A must, either for eating fresh or for freezing. Prepare a patch 3x3ft (1 sq m), in the same way as you would for dwarf beans. Plant the bean seeds individually in pots during the first week of May, and harden off when the plants are 4in (10cm) high. The beans must then be staked, and for this you should prepare wigwams of 8ft (2.5m) canes. The structure should cover the whole of the area of prepared ground, being built from eight canes – this will be very economical in terms of ground covered and a total of two or four wigwams may be built in the corners of the vegetable plot. This method will also reduce the amount of shadow thrown as compared with the alternative way of growing beans, by constructing a row of canes. Only one sowing will be necessary and the beans must be harvested whilst they are still young and tender. Do not attempt to produce the long beans of the show bench.

Beans – Broad

In mild, well-drained areas the hardy 'Aquadulce' variety may be planted as the weather allows from mid-November through to January. Early plantings have the advantage in that they produce a crop which escapes the ravages of the black fly. From February onwards sow one of the 'Windsor' varieties and pick out the growing shoots when the flowers have set. This will not only deter the black fly which will devastate this crop but the shoots may also be cooked and eaten like cabbage. The seeds may either be sown in pots then hardened off and planted out, or the hardy vegetable can be sown straight into the ground providing that it is not waterlogged. In good soil broad beans grow to about 3ft (1m) in height. They do not need staking, but a strong cane should be put at each end of the 6ft (2m) row and two pieces of string tied around the cane in order to form a loop which will support the vegetables.

Courgettes

This is a miniature form of the marrow from which the fruits are harvested when they are 4in (10cm) long. Prepare the bed in the early spring by digging in well-rotted manure; if space is at a premium you may use any site which has become vacant as a result of the first crops, such as lettuce or other saladings grown under glass, having been harvested. Plant the large sunflower-like seeds in pots during early May, and when they have developed two leaves in addition to their cotyledons (the seed leaves), place them

outside during the day to harden off. When there is no longer any danger of frosts plant six plants 2ft (60cm) apart in rows 2ft (60cm) apart. Marrows may be grown in exactly the same way. Two to four plants should be sufficient for the average family.

Cabbage

There are plenty of cabbages in terms of weight in the greengrocers, but shops do tend to have only a small selection of this vast family of vegetables. Many other forms of cabbage are more interesting and present a greater variation in the diet than the ubiquitous forms presented to us on the shelf. All cabbages may be grown by the same method, with the seeds being sown in drills that are ¼in (0.5cm) deep. When the young plants are about 5in (13cm) in height they are placed in rows 24in (60cm) apart, with the individual plants spaced out to a similar distance. Since the average household seeking to provide variety to its diet will not require more than a dozen plants of any single variety, it will be almost as cheap to buy the plants from the local garden centre. Cabbages are gross feeders, and they require a rich soil that is well manured. With summer varieties, but not those which have to stand the winter as the growth which is produced will be too soft and lush, sprinkle a very light dressing of nitrate of ammonia in a circle 6in (15cm) from the stem. This will produce monster specimens. Some of the types that you might choose to grow are white sprouting broccoli, purple sprouting broccoli, calabrese, spring greens, 'January King', 'Christmas Drumhead', cauliflowers and brussel sprouts.

Celery

Celery is an expensive vegetable to buy, and it may be eaten either raw or cooked. Most people prefer the blanched to the self-blanching varieties. Prepare a trench as described for dwarf beans. Sow seeds in potting compost in

77

heat during late March to early April. Harden the plants off when they are 2½–3in (6–7cm) in height. When there is no danger of frost, plant out in two rows in the trench with the individual plants 8in (20cm) apart. When the plants have reached 10in (25cm) in height they should be blanched. Tie newspapers around the plant and earth up. Alternatively, they may be covered with a collar made from a land drain or similar.

Globe Artichoke

This seldom-grown plant reaches almost 6ft (2m) in height and yields a profusion of silver-grey foliage, making it the ideal background plant for the herbaceous bed. If space is short, serious thought should be given to including it in the decorative part of the garden where it will certainly not be out of place. The flower heads, used either as a vegetable or as part of a floral decoration, are a bonus, added to which the young shoots may be cooked and eaten like asparagus. This perennial requires a rich, deep, open soil. Plants should be set out in April and no crop should be taken until the following year. Propagation is by means of root cuttings, which should be potted up in the autumn, and placed in the frame for planting out during the following spring.

Mangetout

This delicious vegetable is another variety that is rarely found in the shops, and it may be grown by the general method adopted for all peas. Prepare a drill 2½in (6cm) deep in rich soil during the early spring. Scatter the seeds on the top of the drill in April, cover with soil and netting to ensure that the birds do not take the seeds, and provide some slug pellets. Mangetout will grow to nearly 6ft (2m) and it will be necessary to provide some support – this may be a net, canes or the traditional birch or hazel pea sticks. Harvest the young tender pods in July and August.

Roots

All root crops are grown by a similar method, but with the small garden you are unlikely to have room for more than a few varieties. Roots prefer a light soil, which has been manured the previous year. Never manure the year that you intend to plant roots. As the root seeds (which are only very small with a small supply of food) will be planted directly in the ground it is important that the seed bed has a fine tilth and does not consist of heavy clods of earth. Break up the soil with a rake until this fine state is achieved. Plant the seeds in drills no more than ¼in (0.5cm) in depth during April. This is a good rule of thumb, as the soil is seldom sufficiently dry to plant before this time and any delay means that the plants will not benefit from the maximum growing period which is the result of the longer days approaching the summer solstice. When the plants are about 2in (5cm) high, begin to thin them out. Thinning out, always taking the weakest plants away, should continue until the mature plants are about 4in (10cm) apart. The thinnings of roots such as carrots may also be used in the kitchen.

Spinach

Rich in iron, carotene and vitamin C, this vegetable deserves to be more popular. If you find the flavour of the annual spinach too strong, cultivate one of the perennial versions.

Sow the large seeds into a well-drained soil in a ½in (1cm) deep drill in April, and for succession throughout the spring until July. Unless the plants are allowed to become too dry, when they will prematurely run to seed, the first sowing will usually last into the winter. When you harvest the leaves take only a few – this will encourage the plants to crop again. Perennial spinach can be used in the kitchen in three ways – the leaves and stalks may be cooked and served together; the leaves may be removed from the stalk and puréed; or the stalks alone may be cooked and served in a similar way to asparagus.

Crop Rotation

It is often thought that crop rotation is essential for successful vegetable growing. With a small plot it is often impractical, and the better approach is to manure the plot regularly and grow the vegetables in the same position. In this way you will gradually build up the soil fertility. The only crop which may present problems is cabbage, which will not grow well if the ground has become infected with club root, in which gnarled growths appear on the roots. If you encounter this problem you should not grow cabbage on that particular site for at least three years.

THE FRUIT GARDEN

Grapes and Winemaking

Orchards are uneconomical in terms of space and there is no place for them in the modern garden, but there are nevertheless several positions within a larger garden scheme that are not fully utilised, and these can be adapted for the growing of fruit. One fruit crop that we should all seek to grow is the grape. Outdoor varieties other than those intended for winemaking do not usually ripen satisfactorily. The best variety you can use is 'Black Hamburg' which has been with us for several years. This is a vine which does not require heat and is ideally suited to growing under glass, either in a greenhouse or conservatory. The roots will withstand British winters, and may be planted outside the conservatory while the stem is trained through a hole bored in the structure about 24in (60cm) above the ground. The vine is allowed to grow up to the level of the roof and then it is stopped. The stopping will induce shooting and two shoots should be trained in opposite directions across the roof of the conservatory. The vine will produce shade in the conservatory and make its use as a sun lounge very pleasant.

Grapes may also be grown and trained on a framework of wire stretched between poles, but you are unlikely to produce sufficient grapes to make your own wine – it will take from 10–20lb to make one gallon (2–4kg to make one litre), and each vine may yield only about 4½lb (2kg). If you want to produce a small quantity of your own wine then you can grow a wine variety of grape along the south side of your house, perhaps in place of a Virginia Creeper or similar wall-covering plant. The grape functions very well in this capacity and the fruit can be considered as a bonus. All of the varieties that survive the British climate yield light table wines. However, you must remember that the United Kingdom is at the furthest northern extremity of the grape-growing region and success in this country will depend upon each micro-climate.

Growing Methods

Dwarf rootstock fruit trees will allow the production of some fruit from tubs, but such trees seldom yield large crops and, unless you particularly want to grow fruit in a confined area, they are probably better ignored. Preferable are the cordon and espalier growing methods, since all that they require is a framework. This may be a free-standing structure which can then act as a screen.

Protection

Fruit is particularly enjoyed by birds, and if you live in an area where birds are a problem, then it will be necessary to build a cage to protect your trees. Such cages can be unsightly but they do need to be about 6ft (2m) in height to enable you to work inside them comfortably. Protected fruit trees are better sited together with the vegetables in the functional area of the garden, but if there is no vegetable garden, you will need to screen the cages with shrubs. If the garden is on a slope, there will be far less of a problem – providing you can find a south-facing slope, the fruit garden may be sited at the lowest level in the dip away from the house. Depending on the degree of slope, the fruit trees will be hidden from view.

Varieties

The varieties of fruit that are grown will be a matter of personal choice, but all types from the soft fruits — red, white and black currants, raspberries, blackberries and gooseberries — will give worthwhile crops, especially if they are mulched in the spring with a little well-rotted compost or horse manure.

If you have a cold frame you will be able to grow cantaloupe melons. The seeds should be brought on in gentle warmth in early May and can be planted out as soon as there is no longer a danger of frost. Alternatively, this fruit is another subject for a cold greenhouse.

Strawberries may be grown in pots, up to 3ft (1m) in height. The pots, filled with potting compost, are planted with about a dozen plants in holes in the side of the container. This arrangement is equally suited to patio or cottage-type garden, and more than one container can be used. If you plant them with different varieties and take them into the greenhouse to be brought on at the beginning of the season, it is possible to harvest strawberries right through from May to October. Wild alpine strawberries such as 'Baron Solemacher' are easily raised from seeds, and make excellent edging plants for both formal and informal flower borders. The fruits are about the size of a fingernail and are delicious sprinkled with sugar and eaten with fresh cream. They are considered by many to be of a superior flavour to the larger varieties, and they can also be used to make a superb liqueur.

THE HERB GARDEN

In considering any scheme for landscaping the role of the garden in relation to the house and family as a whole must constantly be borne in mind. Nowhere is this more important than in the relationship between the kitchen and the garden. Today we are far more fastidious about what we eat and the surplus of food which is now available means that we have to be tempted before we will eat. Moreover, our ideas on nutrition are changing, and we are turning away from our 'traditional' foods and choosing to eat those which are higher in dietary fibre and reducing drastically the amount of meat in our diet. In the Middle Ages it was necessary for completely different reasons to make the food taste better, and we are again turning to spices and herbs to provide interest and excitement in our meals. Unfortunately many of the flavourings that herbs contain are essential oils. These are liquids and as such they are lost, at least in part, in the drying process which is usually used to preserve herbs. The best herbs may make all the difference between a top-quality dish and something less good, and the only practical way to obtain them is to grow them yourself.

A garden of herbs should be sited as near to the kitchen door as is possible, otherwise inclement weather will discourage you from gathering them. For such a premium site the herb garden will have to compete with patio, perfumed garden and even a paved area, but the wise gardener will allow the herbs the choice of locations. In addition to being near to the door the herbs require a well-drained site which receives direct sunlight. Herbs will more than repay the special treatment, with their variety of shape and colours, ranging from the blue of thyme to the global mauve flowers of chives (a relative of the decorative alliums that we grow in the bulb gardens), and a fragrance all their own. Little day-flying moths, butterflies and other insects will provide constant movement around the plants.

There are several designs for herb gardens, and many of them very sophisticated. However, the best for the small garden is a design similar to that used for herbaceous beds, with a gradation of heights from back to front. The choice of herbs should be a culinary rather than a horticultural decision, but this does not mean

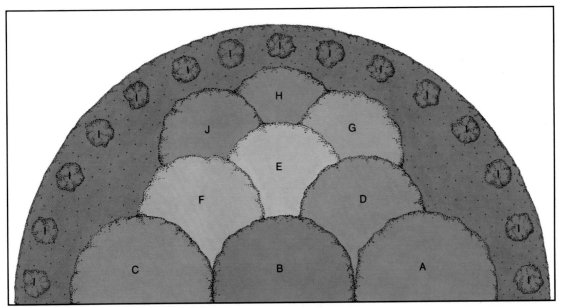

Choice of Herbs

Name		Flowers	Status	Propagation
A	Fennel *Foeniculum vulgare*	Yellow; late Aug	Perennial	Seed or roots during March
B	Rosemary *Rosmarinus officinalis*	Light blue; May to June	Shrub	Hardwood cuttings July to Sept
C	Dill *Anethum graveolens*	Yellow; July to Aug	Annual	Seeds in March
D	Sage *Salvia officinalis*	Violet; June to July	Shrub	Hardwood cuttings July to Sept
E	Basil *Ocimum basilicum*	White; Aug to Sept	Annual	Seeds May
F	Marjoram *Origanum onites*	Mauve; June to Aug	Perennial	Plant division
G	Chive *Allium schoenoprasum*	Mauve, globular	Bulb	Plant division
H	Thyme *Thymus vulgaris*	Mauve; July	Perennial	Plant division
I	Parsley *Petroselinum crispum*	—	Biennial grown as an annual	Seeds early April
J	Mint *Mentha* sp	Range of colours; Aug	Perennial	Root division

Fig 55 Basic layout of a herb garden. The shape may be the basic half-circle or any basic shape which fits into the overall scheme, and it may be changed considerably to blend in with the design. The individual choice of herbs will obviously vary according to taste.

Fig 56 The herb garden provides beauty and fragrance as well as being a source of produce for the kitchen.

that purely decorative plants cannot be included should you want them. For a layout involving the most popular herbs see Fig 55.

Bay trees may be grown separately either in an open site, or more practically in a large tub.

Many cottage gardens included a herb path, consisting of pieces of crazy paving in between which were planted some of the most fragrant herbs, such as thyme. These survive being lightly trodden on and the resultant bruising of the leaves yields a rich perfume.

82

CHAPTER 7

The Patio

Of all the garden styles none is more universally applicable than that of the patio. A patio may often be included in the area between a house and a large garden, although it would be incongruous to introduce into it any scheme which had pretensions towards a cottage garden, and it is essentially a means of dealing with relatively small areas. Although it requires very little maintenance it is not a suitable way of dealing with the whole of a garden but even with the largest of plots there is a place for the patio which creates a horticultural 'no man's land', part house, part garden. In a small town house the patio may be the whole garden, and if your garden is given over to or includes a swimming pool, a patio will effectively deal with that space which surrounds the water. Patios can also be constructed on a roof garden in the city.

The name 'patio' is Spanish in origin and originally meant a large spacious courtyard. In terms of landscaping the word patio is used to describe a garden in which none or very little of the soil is exposed at ground level, and in recent years the style has been used to landscape pedestrian precincts and shopping malls. It is unfortunate that very few patio owners realise what can be achieved with this type of garden, the range of flowers that can be grown and the containers in which they may be housed. Many prefer to think of the patio in its simplest form as a paved area to which containers are added, in which flowering plants in conventional flower pots are grown. The patio is a sun-trap, and an area for people to relax in, so you must make sure that when you site it, it is in full sunlight. In the summer the patio may be more 'house' than 'garden' and consequently it is advisable to site it

actually against the house. The door, or preferably French windows, if you have them, should open straight on to the patio. Bearing this in mind, determine the position of the sun and decide on the best place to construct the walls so that the area will be bathed in sunlight for the longest period of the day. It is not possible to avoid having some areas in the shade, but these should be kept to an absolute minimum. Remember that one of the great pleasures of a patio will be dining out on a summer's evening, when the lengthening shadows will have their most profound effects. South-facing slopes will present no problems, but it is the east-to-west elevations that will require extra care. Another factor that must be considered is privacy, for example, if you wish to sunbathe unobserved. A wall strategically placed will conceal the prostrate form and not block out the sunlight, providing that it is no more than 3ft (lm) in height.

PATIO CONSTRUCTION

Size

Where a patio is built adjacent to a house, with another garden beyond it, all too frequently it is made far too small. It should be realised that the patio is a complete garden in its own right, and represents a good way of dealing with the area that past generations always thought of as the back yard. Where possible, room should be left for garden furniture, as this will allow you to enjoy the patio to the full. If two gardens are to be created on the same site, there should be a difference in the levels of the two components.

Fig 57 The extended house (see Appendix I). The conservatory provides an indoor garden, while the small forecourt outside serves as an area in which to work or dine.

Fig 58 A small urban garden in which a patio is being erected.

Fig 59 The garden in Fig 58 with its patio completed. This area will require only the minimum amount of maintenance, and an instant garden with constant changes may easily be created by bringing container grown plants into the patio.

The Patio Floor

The floor of the patio requires careful planning. Paving slabs should be used, and these may all be of the same size and colour, or they may be of different colours, or different sizes and colours from which patterns can be made. Do not underestimate the importance of mosaic, but avoid patterns that are too complex and do not use more than three different colours in the floor layout. Whilst the pattern in which the slabs are to be laid may appear simple, it should be carefully plotted. Again, forward planning will save you considerable time and eliminate expensive mistakes if any of the slabs need cutting. When laying slabs for the patio, ensure that there is a very slight drop away from the house – 2in (5cm) will be sufficient for virtually all plots. This is important as with heavy rainfall several litres of water will fall on to the surface area, and this must all be made to move in one direction, away from the house and not towards it. Those slabs that run parallel with the house should be level, and laid on a bed of sand 2in (5cm) deep. Gaps for planting equal to a whole slab may be left, but at a ratio of no greater than one in six. You must also take care that they are not so far from the house as to be acting as a

natural drain which could create an unsuitable environment for the plants. Where there is danger of excess water, extra broken bricks or other drainage material should be included in the area to be planted.

The slabs should be grouted in with a stiff mixture of 3 parts sand to 1 part cement. Always work with a piece of cloth to hand in order that you may clear away any of the mixture that spreads over on to the slabs themselves. If it is allowed to dry, it can prove extremely difficult to remove.

A change in the style and texture of the patio floor can be created by leaving a gap (as described above), and filling it with very large pebbles placed on their sides. These are then cemented into position with the grouting mixture. When selecting the pebbles ensure that they are about the size of a hen's egg, and that they match in terms of size, colour and shape. When laying the pebbles check frequently with a spirit level that the stones are being set in a flat position.

Patios are essentially open structures, but they nevertheless possess their own architectural style. This openness should be reflected in the blocks which are used to construct the boundaries and any partitions which will act as separators from the rest of the plot. These bricks can act as a storm break, providing limited protection from frosts and the leaf burn which can ensue, yet still allow sufficient sunlight through so that you don't have an area of total shade. Where the development is at ground level (not in a roof garden, where care must be taken to make sure that the weight does not damage the structure of the house) a sunken pool will add another dimension. It should be created with a liner, using the same general method as for ponds (see page 65). Overlap the sides with 6in (15cm) of paving slabs to form an area in which the fish can shelter from the sun.

Terracing

Terracing a patio will provide extra mass, and the smaller the area is the less change in height there will need to be to retain the balance. Only 6in (15cm) can be quite effective in the smallest patios, with pro rata level changes for the larger area. Larger gradations in size should be accomplished in three or even four steps. The two-level patio offers an opportunity to include moving water in a more adventurous way. Two pools, one at the edge of the higher level and one at the lower, may be constructed. The water can be circulated by means of a submersible pump, with plastic tubing carrying the water from the lower pool to the higher. A jet spray may also be included to create a fountain effect, and in the higher pool the edge of the upper terracing should be modified to function as a tumble tray.

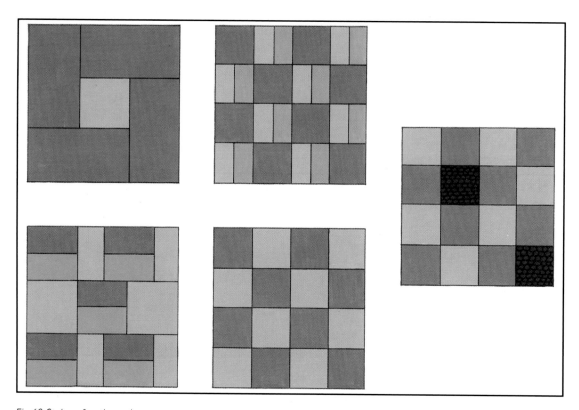

Fig 60 Styles of patio paving.

Fig 61 Styles of patio blocks.

Remember that with smaller moving pond systems (which are the only systems that will fit in most patios), it is impractical to attempt to keep fish, as they require still water and cannot survive in turbulent conditions.

Raised Beds

The raised bed comes into its own in the patio, and should be thought of as a large flower pot that is permanently in position. There is no restriction on the number of these structures, but you should not over-crowd the patio as spaciousness and a feeling of openness are its most important elements. Raised beds should be between 2½ and 3ft (75–100cm) tall. A patio is more of a living floral display than a flower garden in the sense that, with the greatly reduced flowering space, there is no room to allow the plants to complete their whole cycle. They are displayed only during their flowering period and then discarded, or set aside and maintained in a nursery area – but this is all that is required in the modern garden. Where once it was considered a virtue to retain plants for years – the 'waste not, want not' philosopy – today not only do we have far better methods of raising plants, but they are also relatively cheap, so retention of the burnt-out plants is no longer necessary.

With all but the smallest gardens, it is essential to set aside a preparation area in which there is at least a very small greenhouse, which may be either cold, cool or warm. Depending upon the temperature at which they are maintained, greenhouses can open up a completely new range of possibilities and there is no reason why any gardener should not extend his activities to include the growing of exotic subjects. This is perhaps the one area of horticulture where the large plot owner has virtually no advantage over the owner of a small patio. Good hot-house collections of some of the most difficult subjects are successfully grown in greenhouses built on roofs in inner cities. You could just purchase patio subjects when they are required, but this can be very expensive!

PLANTING

If you have left spaces in the patio floor for planting these should be excavated to a depth of 12in (30cm), then filled to a quarter of this depth with broken bricks to act as drainage, and filled with a mixture of equal parts loam, well-rotted farm yard manure (sterilised spent mushroom compost and dried manure used to the manufacturer's instructions are suitable substitutes), and grit. Any summer bedding subjects of your choice that will provide a season-long expanse of colour may be planted in the miniature bed. These are then replaced with bulbs and annuals to provide the spring display. If you choose subjects such as wallflowers and hyacinths you will be able to enjoy their perfume as well as their range of colours the moment you step outside the door. The same principles apply with the raised beds and with mobile containers, such as half beer barrels, that can be used to produce the same effect. It is also possible to buy a whole range of terracotta planting bowls, and these now come in a very wide variety of designs, ranging from the familiar wheelbarrow plant holders to sculptured pots, with strategically-placed holes for the plants to tumble down the sides as well as the open top.

Home-made containers, too, may be prepared from any mould, and you may let your imagination run wild, using a mixture of 1 part cement to 1 part peat and 2 parts sand. The peat effectively produces a neutral brown-grey coloration that will blend with most backgrounds. A useful trick is to wash the outside of the container with milk – the small quantity that remains on the side will sour and the resultant acid conditions will encourage the growth of mosses and other simple forms of plant life on the sides of the pot to give the impression of age and maturity. Once you have decided on either the red-brown of the terracotta, or the grey cement, do not mix the two styles. Any mixture of styles in the patio will be readily obvious, and a loss of consistency in such a small area will result in an untidy appearance. Omit any container that does not fit in with the whole, however much it may appeal to you. The demands of space are such that the growing areas are strictly limited, so you must be ruthless in your choice.

All the contributing factors for your patio – slabs, the type of plants and the containers that they will be grown in – must be carefully considered at the planning stage.

SINK GARDENS

One of the most interesting features that can be created in a patio is a sink garden. This is more than a simple container for growing plants – as the name implies it is a whole garden in miniature, in which small subjects, such as tiny roses and bonsai can be planted, or more simply a miniature rockery specialising in the soil-clinging alpine subjects can be created. You will need a container that is at least 9in (20cm) in depth. Large, old, glazed stoneware sinks are ideal, but they are now a thing of the past and to find a good example you will have to wait until an old house is being demolished. It does not matter how much the glazing is cracked or damaged – you are going to have to remove it carefully anyway. The sandstone colour that will be exposed is unlikely to blend with the patio, so roughly cover it with a fairly firm mixture of peat and cement. It should be moistened just sufficiently to remain on the sides of the sink. Do not smooth, but allow it to dry as rough cast, since you are attempting to give the illusion of natural stone. Treat with milk, and then place the sink on four bricks in such a way that they cannot be seen.

Leave the drain-hole free, then place pieces of broken brick around it to a depth of 1½–2in (4–5cm). Cover the hole with a piece of broken flower pot, followed by a mixture of 2 parts loam to 1 part medium-sized grit and 1 part peat. An alpine garden will not need the richer mixture of the other pots which are yielding a mass of flowers and greenery and which in terms of production are at a maximum. However, it will

need some additional plant nutrients, so to each two buckets of growing medium mix in a handful of 'Growmore' or other general-purpose fertiliser. Avoid fertilisers that are too high in nitrogen as these will only favour the production of large quantities of green material and are most suited to vegetable growing.

INSTANT GARDENS

Instant gardens created indoors, in which an area that is not normally given over to horticulture becomes a mass of flowering blooms, are a familiar sight at banquets and receptions. The gardener can create the outdoor equivalent, in which container-grown plants are brought into display only when they are at the peak of perfection. Providing that you have sufficient greenhouse back-up, there is no reason why you should not change displays as frequently as you wish. One method which is becoming increasingly popular is to grow the majority of the plants in plain flower pots, and then place the plants inside larger and more spectacular patio containers. The flower pots will not be visible, being positioned below the level of the lip of the decorative pots or urns, and you can change them around with ease, choosing each plant in your display individually for quality. Plants used in this way can be introduced in their prime and then removed before they begin to lose their ability to produce blooms. Colour schemes may be co-ordinated, and displays and designs may be created to produce the living equivalents of floral decorations.

The instant garden has many advantages over floral decorations – primarily, you do not have to display blooms that are drooping, as cut flowers tend to do very quickly; also, your instant garden can be a success both inside and outside, with the pots being brought into the house for short periods. The conditions in our houses are seldom conducive to plant growth and in the majority of instances when we bring plants inside as pot plants they begin to die. However, by extending the theory of patio gardening to the inside of the house, we may maintain a constant supply of fresh house plants, and this is particularly true of the summer months. Do remember that the dry heat of central heating systems is the greatest killer of house plants.

Patios should include some subjects which give a consistency to the garden, and provide a green colour to remind the viewer that it is first and foremost a garden, giving an impression of permanence. When it acquires height, *Cupressus* appears majestic and, if it is strategically placed, it will add to the general ambience of the garden. Box, *Acer palmatum* and other small trees and shrubs are all equally well suited. By placing the trees in large tubs, such as beer barrels cut in half, you move them about like furniture until the sought-after illusion is created. Yet they still have sufficient size and presence to give an impression of permanence. By moving around many of the features of the patio, new vistas may be constantly created. Unlike other gardens, the patio need never be static.

FRUIT TREES AND VEGETABLES

Within all of us there is a desire to grow at least some of the food that we eat. For many it can be no more than a token gesture, but that gesture is extremely important. In the patio it is possible to cultivate a whole range of fruit trees in which the popular forms of such old favourites of apples and pears are grafted on to dwarfing rootstock. Cherries, plums, gages, grapes and nectarines can all be grown on the patio. Wherever possible the patio should be south-facing in order to catch the early morning sun, and this will provide a back wall against which it will be possible to grow exotics, such as peaches or nectarines, especially in the south and in sheltered parts of the country. Leave a space in your paving equivalent to one slab, next to the wall. Plant the fruit tree in this area between November and early March, and train by the espalier method. Quick-maturing

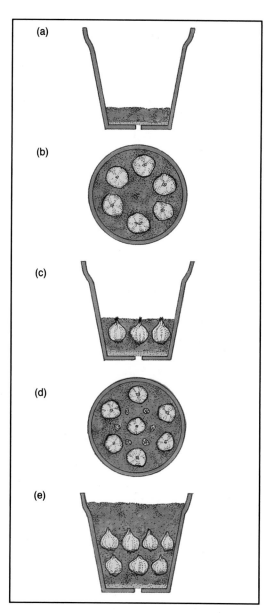

Fig 62 Planting daffodils for patio displays. (a) Place about 2in (5cm) of bulb fibre in the container. (b) Place 4 or 6 (depending on what the pot will hold) daffodil or narcissus bulbs in the bottom. (c) Cover with bulb fibre so that only the tips of the bulbs protrude. (d) Plant a second layer of bulbs between the heads of the first and cover with bulb fibre. (e) The resultant packing of the bulbs will produce a profusion of blooms from the container.

crops, to provide lettuce, radish and other saladings (which must be fresh), can also be grown on the patio in flower beds. Perhaps the most popular of all crops for the patio is the tomato, which may be grown in pots, or like any of the saladings, in growing bags. The largest crops will come from the standard varieties such as 'Alicante' or 'Moneymaker'. If you do not wish to grow these, you should consider 'Gardener's Delight', which will give you up to sixty small tomatoes on one truss. Tomatoes come in a variety of sizes and shapes, and there is now even a miniature variety called 'Totem', which does not need staking and which is ideal for growing on a patio.

HYBRID GARDENS

There are very few gardens that rely on just one landscaping principle; more often they will combine two or more main ideas. The patios that we have considered are those of the smooth man-made concrete slabs and blocks, with mainly terracotta or cement plant containers. Man-made building materials can be selected to blend with each other and to harmonise with the brightest-coloured and largest-flowered plants. Another style of paved garden can be made from sheets of natural rock — unlike slabs, they have no smooth surfaces, and no sharp angles, but rather they are made of rock whose strata is different depending on the angle from which you look at it. Such materials owe more to an alpine landscape than they do to a Spanish courtyard, and look better with the natural plants whose genetics have not been manipulated by man. However the principles and method of gardening are the same as those used on the patio. Such an approach can be very effective in a front garden, where slabs offer no contrast or break from the unending expanse of the other man-made materials which make up the road. Patios can also be used successfully in front gardens although those arrangements requiring privacy will no longer be practical. The garden in the front of the house will have to compete with functional areas — the driveway for the car, and the path to the front door. For a successful patio it will be necessary to separate the garden from these areas, and this can be achieved by raising the level of the patio by about 10in (25cm). Make sure that the paths and drives are laid with a slight slope so that the surface water can gravitate away to a suitable drain. A short hedge will symbolically separate the various parts of a garden as effectively as a screen, and without any of the problems of blocking out light or obscuring views that such a structure might create in such a confined space. Choose subjects such as lavender, which provides flower and fragrance throughout the summer, rosemary, or box, which can be trained and trimmed into topiary sculpture should you wish. Walls may be similarly used but be careful not to create a stark landscape. Too much rock material can be over-bearing, especially against the background of the road. Where walls are used it is important that they are of the double type, with plants growing out of the top, to modify the effects of the stone and the road beyond.

HANGING BASKETS

Hanging baskets allow us to display plants that are essentially low-growing at any height we choose. Suspended displays are bright subjects, often with clashing colours of reds, blues and yellows, and they are the feature that the eye will pick out, the gem against the man-made landscape. As they cover such a small area in a relatively drab background they appear as an oasis of colour, rather than being gawdy or conflicting with their surroundings.

To Make a Hanging Basket

The baskets themselves come in two types — the types with filled-in sides, which are simply suspended flower pots, and the true baskets consisting of a strong wire bowl attached to a

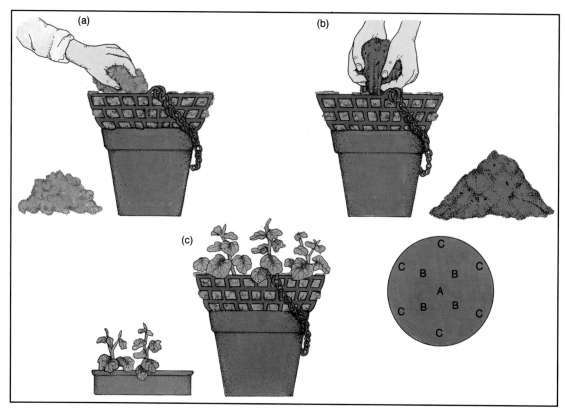

Fig 63 Making a hanging basket. (a) Place moss inside the basket so that no gaps are left. (b) Fill with proprietary potting compost, or a mixture of equal parts peat, loam and grit to which a handful of general fertiliser has been added (to each bucketful). Water to ensure that the moss retains the compost and thoroughly wet the mixture. (c) Plant up with a selection of suitable plants. For example, A is geranium, tuberous-rooted begonia or fuchsia, B is a petunia and C is a trailing lobelia.

chain. With the latter it is first necessary to line the container with a layer of moss (gathered in any woodland during May, the time of year when the baskets must be made up), and place potting compost inside the basket. Run water into it – not only does this ensure that the soil is completely moist, but it also washes it down into the moss, either making a complete seal, or showing up any area of weakness. If the soil is retained within the basket at this stage it is safe to assume that it will be secure throughout the summer. The aim is to create a pendulous effect, so you should not plant standard subjects but the weeping or trailing forms, with geraniums, begonias and fuchsias being the most popular. One or more of these is planted in the centre of the container, and around these petunias may be placed. These will provide bright flowers throughout the summer. The whole is then finished off with about six plants of trailing lobelia. Hanging baskets are best retained in the greenhouse for a fortnight – not only does this make establishing the plants easier, but the warmer conditions will also produce more rapid growth and bring the baskets into flower earlier. Delay putting the baskets out until at least some of the plants are in flower.

Most hanging baskets can be used to house bulbs during the winter. Plant short-growing subjects – muscari, kaufmanniana tulips and hyacinths – raised in the cold greenhouse. As for the summer baskets, delay putting out until the buds are beginning to burst.

Fig 64 A wide variety of containers may be used to good effect to create spectacular temporary displays of colour. With careful planning, plants on a rotation system may provide colour throughout most of the year.

Siting Baskets

Hanging baskets may be sited in any position where they will receive a reasonable amount of sunlight, as well as the partial shade under a porch where they are simply hung from a screw. To attach them to the side of the wall, where they look particularly attractive, purchase a wrought-iron basket holder. With an electric drill bore a hole in the brickwork (not the mortar of the joints), place a plug in the hole and screw the holder into the plugged hole. It is important that the anchorage is strong as together the pot and container will be heavy.

93

CHAPTER 8

Rock Gardens and Heather Gardens

ROCK GARDENS

With its versatile nature the rock garden, or rockery, which reached its zenith during the Victorian era, is rapidly returning to the urban landscape. In a smaller area it gives the gardener the chance to create a landscape rather than simply house a collection of plants, enabling a worthwhile balance between the organic and the inorganic to be achieved. The true rock garden seeks to imitate alpine conditions, encouraging the cultivation of the wide range of specialist plants that have adapted to the harsh mountain-side environment. Alpines, which may come from any part of the world where there are mountains, are short to enable them to withstand the winds of the high ground. They are also adapted to exposure to the almost day-long mountain sun, but above all they have evolved in the presence of the well-drained conditions of the mountain side. They will survive the worst of our winter frosts but they cannot stand their roots being flooded. The rocks in a rockery will provide the conditions that the plants need, with the necessary drainage and also a very thin layer of moisture adhering to the stones in even the driest periods. This will allow for the small amount of water that is required for the plant's survival.

Very few alpine subjects are difficult to grow – only a few of those that originate from very high altitudes present problems and these should not be confused with the popular, easily-cultivated subjects on sale at the garden centres. Providing you can achieve a well-drained, open site – soaking roots are almost certain death to alpines, as is shade – you will be successful. So do not be tempted to site the rock garden under a tree. There are two classes of rock plant – those which are lime-loving, or at least can tolerate it, and those which cannot. It is important to establish the nature of the rock that you intend to use. Lime may be leached from limestones and you should beware of this, but you are unlikely to experience any problems with acid stone since virtually all plants can survive a slightly acid environment. Because some plants, such as some of the azaleas and rhododendrons, originate from a mountain-side location, it does not follow that they can survive in the present of high pH rocks.

Constructing a Rock Garden

Select a south-facing site in an area of the garden which you expect to receive the maximum amount of sunlight throughout the day (it follows that this site will also receive the greatest amount of sunshine all year round). Ensure that the site is well drained – this will not usually present a problem on either sloping or sandy soils. With heavy clay soils you will need to create drainage, and if you intend to build upon a flat site then it will be necessary to excavate at least 3x3ft (lsq m), and fill this sump with broken bricks or large stones. Sloping sites should include a central structure of drainage material only if you consider the underlying ground to be poorly drained. The topsoil should consist of 1 part leaf mould or peat, 2 parts loam and 1 part grit (all measurements by volume, not weight). Ensure that the loam that you use is of the correct pH, or at least that it has not come from a chalk garden if you intend to grow the lime-hating subjects.

Choice of rock will be dictated to some extent by transport costs, which tend to be very high. Most people will be restricted to the stones which are available in their district — consult the Yellow Pages, and remember to ask the quarrymen whether the cost includes transport and whether you may inspect the load before it leaves the quarry (or at least see a typical load). Unless you acquire good stone your efforts and money will be wasted. Check whether the stone has a grain — if it is a sedimentary rock, as most stone that is used in gardening is, it will almost certainly have a grained structure. Due account should be taken when quarrying is done and the cuts should be made with the grain so that you will be able to have the strata running, as it does in nature, in a horizontal plane. Stone has an eternal appearance and it is an important part of the rockery, far more than just a backcloth. Its selection, therefore, demands as much care and attention as that of the plants. When selecting stones buy the largest pieces that you can, as long as you are able to transport it and lift the rock on the site. Incidentally, at a very early stage you should consider how you intend to transport the rocks — the best way is to carry them with the aid of an able-bodied friend, but failing this you can use a wheelbarrow. One tip: where the rock garden is to be constructed after the lawn has been laid, it will be advisable to lay planks on the grass to form a pathway for the wheelbarrow to ensure that it does not cause ruts in the grass.

One of the commonest mistakes when building a rock garden is to use pieces of rock that are too small. Such structures can never be totally effective — the small stones, as well as not creating the same visual impact, may not retain sufficient moisture for the roots of the plants. Before any rocks are actually moved on to the site, prepare a plan showing the position of each individual stone, giving each a number which can be marked on it in a spot that will not be seen once it is in position. If you are constructing a rockery base on an arc or a horseshoe shape, take the largest piece of rock that you have and place it in the most prominent position in the lowest row. This keystone will form the apex and will be the first to be seen by the observer. Where the layout is to be based upon a straight alignment, the biggest stone should be placed where you want to direct the eye. Place the next largest stone furthest away — the stones may then gradually decrease in size as the shape becomes apparent. The rocks should always be placed like flagstones, with the side with the largest area laid horizontally. After you have constructed the foundation layer, the second layer, set back a step, should be put into position. The rocks must be placed in such a way that they are sloping slightly backwards, or, where this is not possible due to the shape of the stone, they should be laid flat. Under no circumstances should they be allowed to slope forwards as this can lead to small pockets of water accumulating. In a true rock garden the rock contributes to the well-being of the plant, and its role is not purely decorative. Do not stand stones on end in an attempt to use smaller pieces — not only will they give an impoverished effect to the structure, but they will also fail to provide the sought-after environment.

Planting

Until the garden has become established the rain will tend to wash out the soil. To avoid this problem, ram soil into the gaps between the rocks until you have an almost solid structure, and at the initial planting stage do not over-plant. Several of the alpine subjects such as *Alyssum*, *Aubrieta*, *Sedum* and *Gentiana*, are never at their best until they have had the opportunity to grow and spread naturally, with some of the plants cascading over the stone walls. It is important to maintain a sense of proportion as if they are allowed to, some plants will tend to

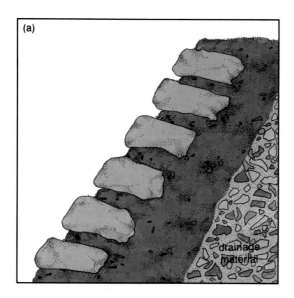 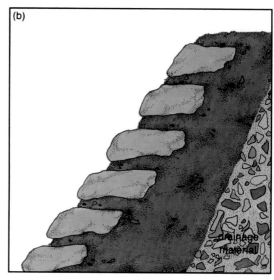

Fig 65 (a) Correct alignment with the rocks sloping backwards. The soil will be retained, and there is very little likelihood of excess water being trapped by the rocks. (b) Incorrect alignment with the rocks sloping forwards. The soil will be easily washed out, and such a structure would trap small quantities of water near to the surface.

dominate and hide the stonework, resulting in much of the painstaking work of construction being wasted.

The rock garden should be approached as a total entity, and plants to give height such as the evergreen conifers may be included to give both a vertical dimension and the mass which is important to all landscapes. Many of the finest alpines are spring-flowering, and where the rockery is part of a larger garden it may be one of the features which creates interest during the early part of the year. It will then successfully provide part of the blended background for the remainder of the year. A rock garden may be included to good effect as part of a housing estate garden or where part of the garden has to be used for a play area. Where space is limited and the rockery has to take on a 'utility' role, plants should be selected in such a way as to extend the flowering season.

PEBBLE GARDENS

Stones are the perfect material for ground cover. They can be used as a blanket to exclude the growth of weeds, and create a virtually main-tenance-free area that requires even less attention than the lawn. Yet this still allows for a far more natural approach to plant cultivation than that of the patio. In the mountains 'scree' is formed from the chippings of rock that are broken away from the hillside as a result of weather and glaciation. This creates a petrified 'sea' slowly travelling down the mountain side. At some points the broken stones move so slowly that they seem to be stationary. Here the small trees of the mountain range, together with certain perennial alpines, will spring up and prosper, nourished by the layer of moisture retained by the stones. Providing the depth of stones is sufficient, seeds (which to the gardener inevitably means weeds) will not grow, as they will not possess the required food supply to enable their roots to penetrate through to the moisture layer. Imitating these conditions represents a good way of dealing with a sloping site, where the owner requires a garden which is not time-consuming, yet does not want the purely man-made appearance of a patio or the particular effect of terracing.

A pebble garden may either be surrounded with grass paths, to give the impression of greenery, or it may be contained within a

Fig 66 A summer house that has been carefully sited to blend in with the surroundings. The beds have been thoughtfully arranged, and are sited within a pebble area – this both achieves a visual effect and reduces the work.

retaining wall, which should be made from rock or stone that matches or blends with the pebbles, and not with bricks which will provide a contrast of natural and man-made materials. In very small areas, if the aspect is correct, it is possible to create a pebble garden between pathways or even a terrace. Dig the area that is to form the garden to a depth of 10in (25cm) – as it is on a slope there should not be any drainage problems. Where the soil is of a good, rich, open loam, since the area will not be requiring rapid growth it is not necessary to include any fertiliser, but bonemeal should be spread at the rate of a handful per sq yd (sq m). If the soil is of poor quality, or is clay-based, dig out the garden to a depth of 10in (25cm) and replace with a mixture of equal parts of good loam, peat and grit. Cover the whole slope with a layer of pebbles to a depth of 4–6in (10–15cm). In addition to pebbles, which are the best

material for this type of garden, you may use road flints, gravel or limestone chippings. Using the latter the soil will become progressively more alkaline and you will not be able to grow any of the lime-hating plants. Check that gravel does not originate from the sea as it will be covered in a thin layer of salt, which could harm some plants.

To plant, dig out an area taking care that the pebbles do not fill the soil as quickly as you are removing it, water well and place established pot-grown plants into the space created. Very carefully replace the stone around the trunk or stems. Short-stemmed subjects may be protected until they become established by a collar placed around them, made from a washing-up liquid bottle, or similar container.

The same principle may be extended to a flat area. Here, however, drainage, which is critical with any type of alpine garden, must be built into the system. Evacuate to a depth of 20in (50cm) and fill the sump formed with broken brick. Cover with a layer of soil followed by chippings as described above.

ALPINE PATHS

Whilst all alpines are not short annual or perennial subjects, many of the best known and most popular forms are. As such they may be grown in the gaps in pathways, as described for herb paths. This is particularly suitable with crazy paving, where the pieces of rock are each creating their own miniature rock garden, providing that there is good drainage under the path. Where an alpine path is being created, it is not necessary to replace the soil under the path. A better approach is to leave gaps in the grouting and force soil into these gaps.

Where there is an established path, carefully remove the cement jointing with a hammer and chisel and replace with sterilised soil. If you cannot obtain sterilised soil you must ensure that the mixture you put into the gaps is free from perennial weeds, especially the stolons of couch grass, as once this becomes established it will intermingle with the roots of the alpine and it will be impossible to remove the weed without pulling out the good plant as well. Until the alpine has had an opportunity to cover all of the available space a very careful watch must be kept for weeds which should be removed immediately. Cracks in pathways attract weed seeds, with any seed landing on the stones being washed into the cracks by the rain.

Alpine paths are not for every garden layout. They are distinctly informal and only really lend themselves to the cottage garden approach, where there is not sufficient room for a rock garden or one is considered inappropriate. Alpine plants will break up the effect of stone and large areas may also be covered in such a way to produce a courtyard. This is another approach to the problem of creating a labour-saving garden that retains its individuality.

HEATHER GARDENS

In recent years a style of gardening based on heather has become very popular and shows every sign of increasing its mass appeal. This is the most universally suitable of all approaches to landscaping the smaller urban plots, yet still retains all of the advantages of 'designer' gardening. Moreover it is an approach which tends to fit in most readily with today's modern life style. It is ideally suited to the person who has little time available for gardening, and to the occupier who is not able to be tied to the home for the regular watering that other schemes demand.

The key to this method of gardening is the heather plant which itself exists in several different species. Cross breeding has resulted in innumerable varieties, and foliage exists in

Fig 67 Heather provides colour and spectacle at a time when it is too harsh for other plants to venture forth.

virtually all tints, from reddish-brown, through yellow-gold, to darkest green. Heathers have a particularly long flowering period and, more importantly, their flowering season is at a time when most other plants have no blooms. By careful selection of varieties it is possible to have blooms from July right through to the following April – such a garden is far less dependent upon the seasons than others. Additional harmonising colour, form and mass may be supplied by planting dwarf conifers. These exist in several forms and, in addition to the new varieties produced by cross fertilisation, there are mutations or freaks, termed 'witches' brooms', which appear from time to time in all plants. These are possibly the result of infection by a virus and have been grafted on to rootstock of a normal form of the same species or similar. These biologically unviable freaks provide many and varied forms, and there is nothing wrong with them, in spite of their origins. The existence of this vast number of both types of dwarf conifer means that, within a very small space, anyone may amass a collection of these interesting subjects. However, it is advisable to seek out a specialist supplier rather than rely on the local garden centre.

The development of form in the horizontal plane, and weed-excluding ground cover, can be achieved by planting *Juniperus horizontalis*. The bluest of all the junipers, this variety has a prostrate mode of growth and can cover up to 6ft (2m) when fully grown. Ground cover is an important feature of this type of gardening – all of the plants have a tendency to spread, and this reduces the need for weeding to a minimum. A variation on this theme is to use dwarf conifers as the only subjects in the bed. This approach is less popular as it involves no flowers, but the dwarf conifers do produce a variety of cones, and some have blue or gold leaves whilst others possess bright red, fawn, or lime green growing tips. They have an advantage over the heathers in that they will grow in most types of soil. The heathers as a group are acid-loving, and whilst some will tolerate a small amount of lime in the soil, none

of them actually *prefer* alkaline conditions, and you will be very limited for choice if you restrict yourself to those which are less fastidious in terms of soil.

If the pH of the soil is above 7.0 dig out the area where the heathers are to be planted and replace with a mixture of loam (not from a chalk-based area), peat and sand. It is wrongly thought that peat is essential for heathers – the result of growing heathers or ling on a soil for centuries can result in the formation of peat, and this is why peat is so often found in association with them in the wild. However, heathers will grow in sand, and only minimal nutrients need be added to the soil – a handful of bonemeal per sq yd (sq m) will suffice.

Rocks

To accentuate the colours, and to achieve a balance between the organic and inorganic, rocks of a buff colour can be included in the initial layout. This helps to provide an instant garden, occupying some of the space, and compensates for some of the young plants, which will not yet be providing full ground cover. The role of these stones should not be confused with that of the stones in the rockery. They are not involved in the actual growing process, and the roots will not be growing under them as they would in the case of an alpine. They may be removed when the total ground cover has been achieved. Consequently, these rocks do not need to be embedded in the soil, and may be smaller. What must be avoided are any rocks of chalk or limestone as the rain will leach the alkali out and this will destroy the lime-hating plants. Colour may be supplied to such systems by means of miniature rhododendrons, miniature daffodils, or gentians, preferably in a manner which retains the effect of bright jewels of colour in succession throughout the year.

99

Trees

The features of such gardens should not necessarily be thought of as permanent. There are some slow-growing conifers which may initially be included in the layout, but which will ultimately grow too large to remain within the heather garden. These trees are too good to be destroyed and because they are small, if not miniature, they make excellent subjects for giving form to the garden as a whole. The secret is to remove the tree whilst it is still small, and you can still comfortably dig out the root ball without damaging the layout of the garden in the process. The tree, which must be moved during the winter months, should be placed in a strategic position in a lawn. Subjects which grow to 6–10ft (2–3m) are ideal specimen trees for even the smallest gardens – average-sized plots will be able to carry a tree of 12–15ft (4–5m). A very effective garden, that blends well with modern architecture, may be achieved from no more than a simple heather garden together with two or three specimen conifers and one dominant larger tree giving both the necessary form and mass. Specimen conifers, especially *pinus*, *picea* and juniper, even in their dwarf forms, have a parkland quality that allows the gardener to create a truly 'landscaped' design in even the smallest areas.

Fig 68 The use of conifers. The form of the beds is in two distinct planes, and the vertical and the horizontal are used to achieve a balance.

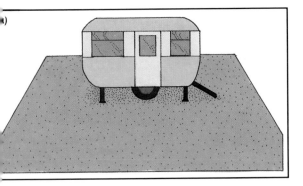

Fig 69 (a) Dealing with a parking or storage area. Here the caravan is an eyesore, a scar on the landscape. (b) Whilst you may be restricted in the buildings that you may erect, you can grow trees and hedges to conceal any view that you wish. Here strategically-placed macrocarpus and a hedge improve the sight. The same principle of planting trees between the unacceptable view and the viewer may be applied to blot out such external objects as gasholders.

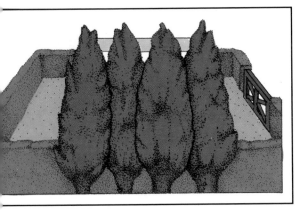

Fig 70 The centre of the lawn can be a suitable place for planting trees but be sure to site them a good distance from the house so that shadows are not cast over the windows.

Siting Trees

The greatest possible care should be taken in the siting of trees — they are permanent features of the garden and you do not often get a second chance when dealing with the large specimens. Lower branches can form a framework and create a view. Equally importantly, they may obliterate a view — a strategically-placed tree can easily hide a caravan or gasholder from the field of vision from the main window of the house. If the position where the tree should be placed is not readily apparent, you should ask a partner to hold a siting pole, and consider the effect from the most important viewing position, with the pole representing the tree placed in all its possible locations. Due regard must be given to the shadow that the tree will throw — it will be equal in length to the height of the tree at midday — and the spread of the roots. Select a site for a tree only after the fullest deliberations — you are going to have to live with it for a very long time.

Using heathers, conifers and grass it is possible to create a garden of minimal maintenance, where little more will be needed than cutting the grass regularly, spring and summer servicing of the lawn, and any necessary pruning of the trees. The latter should be kept to a minimum, but those conifers that you intend keeping in the beds should be shaped and kept within bounds during November to February.

101

CHAPTER 9

Formal Gardens and Jungles

CREATING A FORMAL GARDEN

The formal garden represents the most time-consuming of all methods of landscaping – it requires almost constant attention, and any imperfections will be apparent to the most casual observer. For a start, the lawn must be of top-quality, fine cultivars. You will find it easier to start with turves, which will need cutting up to three times per week with a rotary mower during the most rapid growing season of late spring and early summer. The edges must be razor-sharp and the beds maintained weed-free – because the beds of formal gardens have less plant cover any weeds are immediately obvious. The formal garden requires a geometrical shape. It will have less mass or form, with the emphasis moving towards the colour generated by the flowers, and as such it will demand the purest of forms and the most breathtaking of colours. This has led to the search for better bedding plants that are usually grown as annuals to be discarded when they have finished blooming. To maintain interest all the year round the beds will need to be replanted up to four times a year.

To create a formal garden the various features must be measured accurately, the whole flattened area marked out, the turves laid and the beds constructed. The only element of height which is usually included within the beds will come from standard roses, which are also one of the very few permanent plants commonly used. Their inclusion is 'allowed', partly because of

the reverence in which we hold this flower, and partly because modern cultivars will bloom throughout the summer and maintain interest in the garden. Standard fuchsias which also have a long flowering period, and produce the regal colours of magenta and red, can be included in any scheme too, but there is a disadvantage in that most of the better forms are not really hardy and must be removed and given protection during the winter. Similar difficulties are experienced with tuberous-rooted begonias – in shades of red, pink, yellow and white, these provide limited height but because of their flower form they should not be grown in beds which contain or which are adjacent to roses, with which they will compete unsuccessfully. The fibrous-rooted begonia is a low-growing, single-blossomed form, which can be one of the main plants of the summer scheme.

Summer Formal Bedding Plants

Plants which will bloom from June through to the first frosts – alyssum, antirrhinum, asters, begonias (fibrous-rooted), *lobelia*, marigolds (French and African), petunias, *tagetes*, *salvia*.

Autumn and Winter Bedding Plants

All-year-round pansies and polyanthus (these will only bloom during a mild winter but will be the first to appear during the spring).

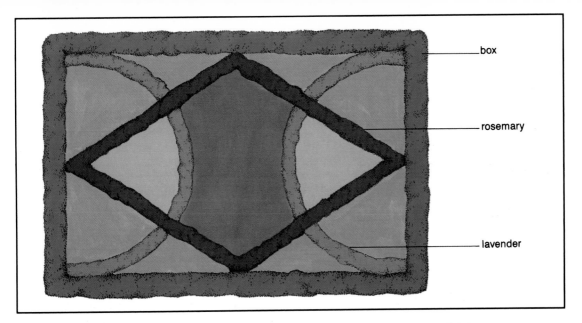

Fig 71 A simple design for a knot garden. When knot gardens were first introduced to Tudor Britain, they were often very large. Small versions are ideally suited as layouts for the modern urban garden. The garden consists of geometrical, often very complicated designs – providing the symmetry is retained, they may be as intricate as you wish. The original elements were constructed from the dwarf hedging plants of the time, but today we have a wider range of plants to choose from. The elements may also be constructed in brick or stone. The spaces in between are planted with either traditional cottage garden subjects or modern bedding plants.

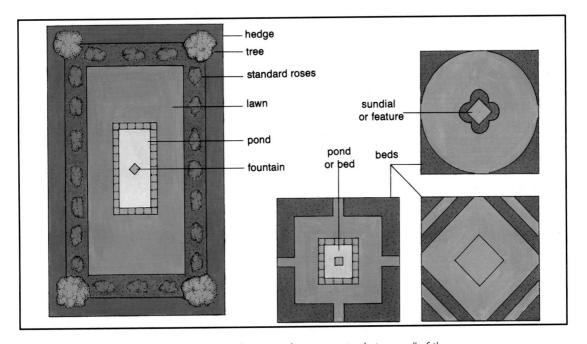

Fig 72 The formal garden. For a formal garden there must be a symmetry between all of the elements of the layout. In the perfect formal garden, each half of a line drawn latitudinally and longitudinally should be the mirror image of the other. This degree of formality for the whole garden is seldom possible, or even desirable, but it is attainable in parts of the garden. A small formal garden may be just one of the elements making up a whole garden, and may be separated from the remainder by a fence or screen.

103

Early Spring Bedding Bulbs

Must be planted under the bedding plants during the autumn. Daffodils, other types of *narcissus*, tulips (the short 'Kaufmannii' or tall 'Darwin types').

Late Spring Bedding Plants

Late tulips (under-planted in the autumn), stocks, pansies, daisies (all transplanted).

TOPIARY

Topiary is one of the oldest of gardening skills, dating back to the time when landscapes had to be created from indigenous plants and the few species that had been imported by the conquerors. The English yew was extremely popular, being one of the few evergreens of a dense compact growth, and together with box was cut into several different shapes. Topiary was an art that had all but died out, with only a few examples remaining and those associated almost entirely with the large gardens. Topiary can, however, be used in the smallest gardens, and it requires far less skill than might be expected. Both box and yew can be cut into simple geometrical shapes, such as squares, spheres and pyramids.

When growing for a lawn it is better to raise the tree in a tub to establish the basic shape. The tubs may be resited from time to time in the garden and be included in a patio garden or as part of a lawn. Transplanting represents no

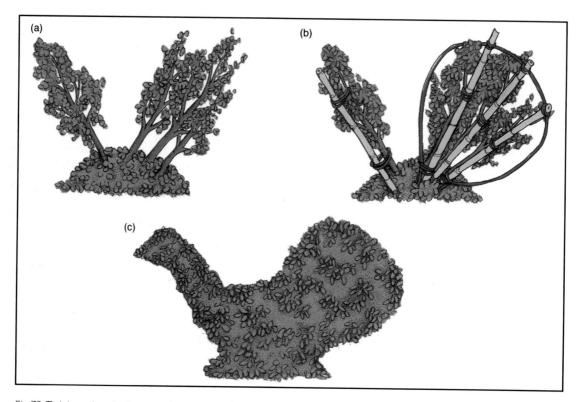

Fig 73 Training a box bush to produce a peacock shape. (a) Separate the growths that will form the tail and the rest of the body (b) Place them in a framework of wire and bamboo, and tie into position. Stop a shoot for the head. (c) Allow to thicken, before trimming to the basic shape.

problem providing that you plant during the winter months and you excavate a hole slightly larger than the root ball of the trees.

Creating Sculptures

When it is about 18in (45cm) high, a pot-grown tree can easily be made into a peacock shape. Prepare a half-circle of ⅛in (3mm) wire with a diameter of 20in (50cm) and with struts of wire and bamboo running from the centre to the circumference. Insert this into one end of the tub. Divide the branches of the mini tree in two and direct one set of growths on to the half-circle, tying into the struts. This will make up the tail of the peacock. Train the other half of the branches or one stout branch (you may have to consider carefully the best way to divide the bush) along a stout bamboo cane set at 45 degrees to the ground. Stop the growth level with the top of the tail. Stopping will encourage other shoots. With secateurs remove all of the shoots except one which will form the break. Trim the bamboo back until it no longer protrudes, and thereafter trim the peacock as the tree grows, tying in any additional shoots. The framework is left in the tree. (See Fig 73.)

Animals may be created on the top of a yew hedge by making an animal shape out of heavy-duty wire with a stout rod in the base. This rod is securely fastened on to one of the main growths of the hedge with plastic baler twine which rots only slowly. The rest of the hedge is kept trimmed, but no cutting of the animal shape takes place until growths protrude outside the frame. They are then cut to shape. Any animal may be created in this way. Do not make sculptures that are too large as it may take a long time for the ugly wire work to become covered – there is no means of speeding up the process.

IN PRAISE OF JUNGLES

Every garden, however small, has a space for a 'jungle' – an overgrown area where nature

Fig 74 A profusion of growth. This apparently informal corner displays a gradual progression in height, providing the impression of mass within the garden.

Fig 75 A glorious jungle of growth with yellow Verbascum magnum, black fennel (Foeniculum vulgare), and pink Malva alcea 'Fastigiata'.

appears to be in complete command, and where man seem to have failed to impose himself upon the urban landscape. Like the rest of the garden, such an area is an illusion. It is not the true natural garden that would spring up as a result of neglect – that would harbour little more than grasses and stinging nettles, and simply advertise the fact that the area had not been looked after. The urban jungle should be completely under the control of the gardener, yet at the same time it must be allowed to develop in a natural way.

Shrubs such as the purple-flowered rhododendrons, and the prickly-leaved, yellow-flowered, *mahonia* are ideally suited to such situations, blossoming in the spring. They simultaneously provide the ground cover that will eliminate the need to weed the area, and the dense mass of undergrowth and top growth which creates the impression of mystery. Such an area will of necessity be robust, providing an irresistible attraction to children, and allowing their imaginations to run riot.

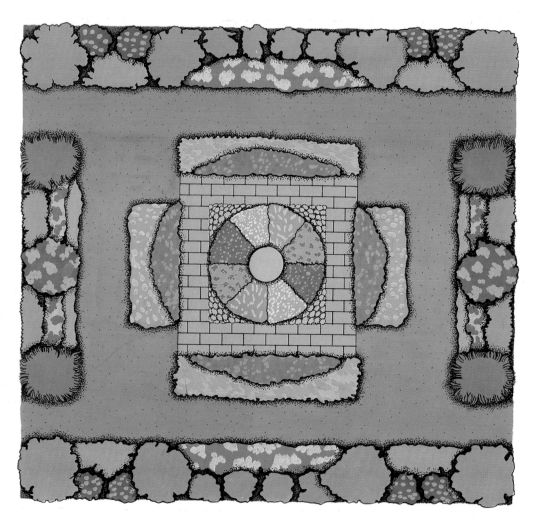

Fig 76 The semi-formal garden allows you to retain some aspects of a more formal design, such as the 'plane of symmetry', yet permits a far greater latitude and variety in the selection of plants.

CHAPTER 10

The Cottage Garden

THE STYLE

The cottage garden differs from the other styles of gardens in that the plants are all-important and all other features are present only in a supporting role. No longer do we consider the marrying together of the organic and the inorganic, instead we have a collection of plants, each one capable of sustaining an interest in itself. We seek to assemble the collection in a harmonious way so that the whole is greater than the sum of the parts. Trellis work and other items give the plants support, but all these are no more than a showcase for the living exhibits. With the profusion of plants in their infinite variety, going into a cottage garden and seeking to study the brick or woodwork is rather like going to a concert and concentrating on the decor of the auditorium! However, this does not mean (in either case) that the supporting features are not important or that they should not be chosen with the greatest care — any failings would be immediately apparent. They should blend unobtrusively into the background, performing their role but never seeking to be apparent.

Cottage gardens are always associated with the countryside, and they certainly evolved in the country because they pre-date urbanisation and the movement of man to the towns. Today there is no reason why cottage-style gardens cannot be developed in town centres, and there are several highly successful examples of this approach to urban gardening. Only the very smallest town-centre gardens — no more than a few square

yards in area — cannot be developed in this way. Such minute plots are the exception rather than the rule and most people will have sufficient space in which to create their plant collection. 'If only I had a larger garden' or 'The garden is too small' are laments that are frequently heard, but you do *not* need a large area. On even the smallest sites interest can readily be created, especially where it is left to the plant to do this. With a small garden you may not be able to afford the room for trees, but mass and height can be created within the individual beds — stately lupins, hollyhocks, flag lilies and foxgloves perform a role similar to that of elms in a parkland, and lesser subjects, such as Canterbury Bells, larkspur and godetia, also give form to individual beds. The cottage garden will bring with it scents which will change throughout the winter months; seeds will be produced in profusion and will attract seed-eating birds; bushes can provide nesting sites; honeysuckle (woodbine to the countryman) or clematis will change the stark walls of the urban jungle to a mass of colour. The case for making a cottage garden in the town centre is perhaps stronger than it is for the green belt.

The style of house is not important with this type of garden — the chocolate-box picture of a thatched cottage with black painted timbers and white plaster work is a contrived view both of architecture and horticulture. On the contrary, the feature that denotes the cottage style above all others is an awareness of height and its effect upon the mass of the site. The cottage garden is

Fig 77 This modern patio garden will eventually acquire a 'roof' as the climbers cover the pergola to create a pleasant area for relaxing.

a profusion of growth — growth which occupies the air, rather than hugging the ground, as is the case with the alpine garden or formal design. The cottage garden is a celebration of flowers and vegetation. Foxgloves and hollyhocks will take the eye upwards, as will climbers on the walls, and the whole design states that the house is secondary to the garden.

SOIL

If you intend to develop an older town-centre site into a cottage-style garden, you should first test the pH. If it is below 5.0, apply lime at the rate of 2oz/sq yd (50g/sq m). Treatment with lime should aim to bring the soil up to the neutral point, but not beyond it. Virtually all of the cottage garden plants can tolerate acid, but they cannot all live in the presence of an excess of lime. Remember that the chemical will take time to disperse through the soils, as it is not readily soluble, and it is pointless re-testing as soon as the lime has been applied. After the soil has been treated, in the first year plant only annual seeds, which are relatively cheap. Their success will tell you whether or not you have a suitable medium for growing the whole range of cottage garden plants. The alternative approach with small sites that may have been subjected to decades of atmospheric pollution is to replace the soil with good quality loam. This can be expensive but it is a sure way of solving the problem.

CLIMBING SUBJECTS

There is often a reluctance to grow ivy and other creepers as it is mistakenly thought that they cause a house to be damp. Many of them, however, have minute aerial roots which actually extract moisture from the wall. To convert a house into a cottage (in the horticultural sense), you need do no more than plant a climber such as a Virginia Creeper. This plant will cover the wall with green leaves in summer (far less effort

Fig 78 Climbing plants can be used to spectacular effect to soften the hard lines of both old and new buildings. The majority of subjects are easy to grow and will spread reasonably quickly.

than painting it!), turning to flame-red in the autumn. Even when it is denuded during the winter, the trunks and branches will continue to create an illusion. All-year-round colour may be provided by ivy, with the variegated variety being particularly suitable. For a less dramatic effect, the golden-berried *Cotoneaster* may be trained up a trellis work on the side of the house, and its buff-coloured flowers will be a bonus in the spring. Also delightful are flowers blooming over a porch — choice of flowers is particularly important, but roses remain the most popular. Today it is possible to obtain a very wide range of roses grafted on to climbing rootstock. When choosing roses intended for planting over a porch, you should pay as much attention to their perfume as to their colour — you will be aware of the scent long before you can see the flowers. Seek out a specialist grower or ask your local garden centre to obtain the variety that you have chosen. You should need only one rose for over the door, but, if you need more than one, do not try to mix colours as it will spoil the effect, which

Fig 79 Colour co-ordination. The gold leaves of Spiraea japonica *'Goldflame' are echoed in Golden Privet (*Ligustrum ovalifolium *'Aureum') and* Robinia pseudacacia *'Frisia' in the background.* Geranium psilostemon *in turn echoes the copper foliage of* Rhus cotinus.

Fig 80 Wall-climbing plants are equally suitable in the town and the country. Here wisteria shows off a twentieth-century house.

should be one of simplicity. You can also train other roses on trellis work around the house, but avoid too much growth on the walls. For example, where you have a background of ivy or Virginia Creeper, do not attempt to grow other climbing subjects unless it is over a protruding porch.

Climbing roses are not true climbers – they will not produce tendrils which will anchor themselves to any support available, but need to be trained and tied into position. One very effective way of combining all of the advantages of this plant is to construct a large pergola-type arch at the entrance to the garden from the roadway. Providing that they are 'dead-headed', climbing roses will provide a profusion of flowers from June until the time that the frosts cut them down in October. In addition to the exterior decoration there will be sufficient left over to keep up an almost continuous supply of cut flowers. Also, in the past, the hips were used to produce a syrup which was particularly rich in vitamin C, or for making a 'nutty' wine similar to a Madeira.

Another climbing subject that is quite outstanding in its beauty is the passion flower (*Passiflora*). This is an evergreen subject which will survive all but the harshest of British winters, and the dark leaves are complemented in the summer by the two-tier passion flower which is said to mimic Christ's crown of thorns. These are followed in the late summer by bright orange, egg-shaped fruits. It is a plant which prospers especially well in the slightly warmer conditions of British coastal towns.

DISGUISING EYESORES

One of the most important aspects of cottage gardening is that there are very few rules, and you may use the plants in unconventional ways that would not be applicable in more formal settings. Sheds and other out-buildings can be successfully covered with a climbing plant such as the clematis, which can be obtained in the widest range of colours, or the lilac-coloured wisteria, both of which will gratefully accept the surface

Fig 81 An arch at the gate gives the first impression of both the house and garden, and provides the perfect support for a climbing rose.

provided. In time the plant will hide most of the building, and will certainly soften the effect of a man-made element in an otherwise natural scene from the day that it is planted. Tree trunks can be extremely difficult to remove, requiring great physical effort, so, rather than attempt to do this, why not plant a clematis alongside, and what was an eyesore and something which needed hiding will become a thing of beauty. An ordinary tree, too, may be enhanced by having a climbing rose or a clematis growing up its trunk and exploding into bloom amongst its lower branches.

FRUIT TREES

The larger cottages of the countryside always had a Bramley seedling apple tree, even where there were no other trees.

In terms of landscaping this tree had to perform all of the functions that you would expect – to give height, mass and form, and to provide shade. Many a happy childhood hour would be spent in this stalwart of the cottage garden, and its lower limbs would more often than not support the ropes of a swing. Bramley trees are monsters that, year after year, produce enormous crops to provide for all your culinary needs, including adequate supplies of an incomparable chutney. As the year turns the apple gradually loses much of its acid during storage and, whilst remaining the perfect cooking apple, slowly takes on a dual role, becoming a dessert fruit that will last until following spring. This truly remarkable tree will continue cropping for sixty to a hundred years, and, should you inherit one, it should be retained at all costs, as the Bramley is without peer as a culinary apple. Do not be deceived by the relative antiquity of the variety – the production of a new variety of apple is still very much a matter of chance and we have still not succeeded (and perhaps never will) in breeding anything superior. Your Bramley tree may also be used to provide excellent support for a clematis or honeysuckle.

The cottage garden allows for the growth of full-sized fruit trees if room permits. Not only are these better croppers but it also allows you to consider growing some of the rarer but nevertheless worthwhile fruits, such as medlars, gages and walnuts.

An alternative approach to the growing of fruit trees is to prune them so that their total spread does not exceed 6ft (2m), and to create a small bed under the trees. Such a small spread will not exclude the light from the plants below and it is possible to create small beds raised above the level of the lawn and to plant them with seasonal subjects.

BULBS

During the autumn under-plant the trees with spring bulbs. The first harbinger of spring during the dull, dark days of winter is the snowdrop, and many grouped together in clumps can produce a most dramatic effect. These are quickly followed by crocuses, daffodils, narcissi and the other bulbs of spring, right through until the blue, white and pink bells. All of these are true cottage garden subjects that have stood the test of time and are not just a whim of fashion, and all will require no attention whatsoever once they have been planted. Left to nature they will return with the sun to bloom every New Year. If you grow bulbs in this manner in the lawn, there is a disadvantage in that you cannot cut the lawn until the leaves of the bulb have turned brown. It is

Fig 82 Cottage gardens in mid-summer produce a blaze of colour and a richness of fragrance as well as attracting wildlife.

the leaves that make and store the food which will form the new bulb, and unless all of their substance can be absorbed by the young bulb they will not be able to produce flowers for the next year. This can mean delaying cutting the lawn until well into the season.

DESIGN

Cottage gardens can be built without a lawn, but such an approach should only be used in the very smallest of gardens. In designing the garden it is best to picture the whole area as a lawn and to use this as a blank canvas from which beds can be cut out, and to which trees, woodwork, walls and paths can be added. The beds themselves are of the utmost importance. They must be

planted in such a way that they give the impression of being free-growing, whilst at the same time being under the total control of the gardener. The beds should be sufficiently small to allow the planting operations to be performed from the lawn and paths initially. You are unlikely to acquire all of the plants that you wish to include during the early stage, and the cottage garden should be something which is allowed to evolve anyway. Additional flowers will be collected over the years and room will have to be found for them. The individual plants themselves will increase in size, seeds will fall to the ground and gradually the surface will become covered. One answer is to increase the size of the beds themselves – providing this is done in a symmetrical manner, that is, *all* of the beds (or all of those in a similar position or field of vision) are

Fig 83 The importance of bed shape. Where a bed is to be cut into the lawn of an informal garden, a kidney or other similar shape is preferable to a more geometric design.

increased, it will not affect the balance of the garden. This is only possible if the beds are kept relatively small when the original garden is constructed. Always remember when cutting beds out of a lawn that they can be easily enlarged at some later date, and that it is virtually impossible to reduce them.

There is no reason why you should not move the plants from one bed to another. It is highly unlikely that you will get all of the plants into their ideal situation at the first attempt, and you may wish to rearrange the garden to form different groupings of your materials. Moving plants will present no problems, providing you do it during the winter when the plant is naturally dormant and its water requirement is at a minimum. To ensure a successful transplant there must be as little root disturbance as possible – ideally the

plant should not be aware that it has been moved. This can only be achieved if a sufficiently large rootball containing the majority of the roots of bushes and shrubs, is removed. Do not attempt to move trees unless they are dwarf conifers, or are only in their first or second year after planting. With herbaceous subjects the plants may be divided at the same time. This is most easily performed by cutting through the centre of the root with a very sharp knife.

Planning the Beds

Each bed in the cottage garden should have a theme or a common feature. Some of the beds may be timed so that all, or the majority of, the plants burst into flower at the same time. The garden will consist of a series of 'time-capsules'

Fig 84 A profusion of foliage and flowers, including variegated periwinkles, variegated Lemon Balm (Melissa officinalis), pink Claytonia sibirica *and Forget-me-not (Myosotis).*

to be activated by the natural calendar during the months of the year. Other beds may consist of plants which have something in common – a bed made up of just plants with variegated leaves can give the most startling effect during those parts of the flowering season when there is less colour, but when the weather will still encourage us to enjoy our gardens. Other beds may be given over to growing those subjects which will attract wildlife. One or more beds can be used to grow perfumed plants, whose influence will permeate the whole garden and provide that heady scent that makes you aware that you are in a cottage before you have even seen a single plant. One bed may include the herbs. The cottage garden is a total concept – the various components that are so often found in other gardens are all there, but the beds act as a sort of natural 'filing cabinet', a set of self-contained units which collectively form the totally balanced garden.

When planting the beds initially you must be aware of the balances – the balance of colour (see page 47), and the balance of form, which is concerned with the mass of the bed. The bed must have a gradation of height from back to front, but the form should change such that in the plane across the bed there is a gradual narrowing of the mass of greenery and flowers from the front to the back. Irrespective of what small, unobtrusive, yet nevertheless interesting, plants may be included in any collection, it must be possible to absorb the whole visual image just by looking at the bed. There is a panoramic view that is essentially a cottage garden.

Where a hedge is included, this will have to be taken into account when planning the beds. To retain the greatest interest, never plant the same varieties in more than one bed. Each bed should be a self-contained creation of different plants, with no repetition in adjoining displays. More than one plant of the same variety may be

included in a bed, but always go for an effect of grouping. Never plant more than one example of the same variety singly dispersed throughout the bed; instead, bring them together to achieve a dramatic impact, allowing the plants to make a statement. With small groups, include an odd number and plant in a triangular pattern with the apex to the front.

Ornaments

The cottage garden will allow for the use of ornaments, but they must be used sparingly. For example, two pots, one either side of the door like statues at the gates of a city, can be used to house plants which need to be taken inside during the winter. The centrepiece should have a timelessness about it – a bird bath made of cement or a bird table hold their attraction, but for a really 'old-world' effect it is hard to beat one of the traditional pieces of cottage garden furniture, the sundial. One of these can be readily obtained from some of the larger garden centres. Only a very small number of cottage gardens actually possessed beehives, but if you can get hold of one of the old WBC hives from a country market or the classified column of the local paper, paint it and restore it. Even without the bees, it will create the illusion of a rural idyll.

Secret Gardens

The concept of a secret garden appeals to the child in all of us, and nowhere is it easier to produce the effect than in the cottage garden. You need do no more than extend the two beds which are furthest away from the house in a symmetrical manner, so that only the smallest part will be visible from the main window. The roles which such an area may perform are infinite – it can be a wildlife area, a vegetable garden, a fruit garden, a service area (containing green-house, potting shed and compost heap), or play area. More clearly defined secret gardens may be formed by growing a hedge and situating a gate in the middle of it.

Fig 85 (facing page) A stately pond – the stone and verdant backcloth together give a feeling of eternity, while the fountain brings movement into an otherwise static landscape.

Appendices

I THE EXTENDED HOUSE

Sun lounges and conservatories fall half-way between the house and the garden, and as such they should complement both. They represent the most cost-effective way of extending your house, and often they do not even require planning permission. However, you should always check that this applies in your area with the local authority.

Your choice of sun lounge should be based on architectural considerations. Rounded structures, once much loved by our Victorian ancestors, are once again back in fashion – if they are made in mock mahogany, such structures can be chosen to match the door, windows and other house fittings. They are shown to their best architectural effect in terraces or on estates where all the houses are identical, or at least similar in design, where their inclusion will give the house an individuality.

The range of designs of glass home extensions is greater than it has ever been, and it is also possible to buy rectangular lounges with sliding doors, ideally suited to opening out on to the patio or paved courtyard. This is now a highly competitive market, and if you shop around you may be able to find your own designer-made sun lounge at little extra cost.

Fundamentally, your extension will become a 'winter garden' – an area to be enjoyed when there is less interest outside, and when the elements are too harsh for outdoor activity. Moreover, it is a room of the house, so the designer must be concerned with its interior decoration, which will be based on the use of living plant materials. The range is wide, and even

in a relatively small space it is possible to provide tropicals – palms, orchids, ferns and bananas are just some subjects which, when combined with cane or white-painted wrought-iron tables and chairs, will create that effect which is so often seen in glossy magazines.

Sun lounges add an extra dimension to your enjoyment or your living space – they can be used to extend the period when meals can be taken outside the house itself, and they make ideal studies. However, care must be taken in selecting the plants to enhance this room. Several tropicals require high humidity and, whilst it is certainly possible to achieve this, it is not conducive to happy human habitation. During their season, gloxinias, cinerarias, begonias, cyclamens and azaleas will all provide the house with colour, but it can be difficult to create the right conditions for these plants indoors, and they do not always prosper because of the micro-climate of the room.

You do not have to heat a conservatory, but if you do you can use it as a study or lounge at those times of the year when the sun is not warm enough to heat the room, and the range of plants that you can raise in it will be greatly increased.

II WILDLIFE IN THE GARDEN

Birds, butterflies, even the occasional dragonfly all create movement and are a constant source of interest. In the unplanned garden they will be chance arrivals that make a fleeting visit and disappear from whence they came. However, careful garden design can, by providing the plants

Fig 86 Water is a vital ingredient in attracting all kinds of wildlife to the garden.

that attract them and the necessary shelter, persuade more wildlife to visit the garden and remain longer. Some will even take up residence and breed in the garden.

Many people are deterred from considering wildlife gardening, believing that it involves giving over patches to stinging nettles and other weeds. You can if you wish plant wild flowers – those of the meadows and chalk downlands can now be bought from seedsmen – if space allows such areas can be hidden away in a secret garden. Even a modest ecological garden requires careful planning, and you will need to plant the correct flowers to attract the butterflies that you are seeking. For example, the Blues of the chalklands and the Marsh Fritillary require plants from vastly different habitats and you will never persuade them to co-exist in the same area, any more than you can make lime-loving plants grow alongside the azalea. With wildlife you must decide which forms you wish to attract into your garden and set about creating the environment that they seek. Even if you just attract the adult forms, the female will probably find weeds on which to lay her eggs, on a piece of rough ground or an unkept plot within butterfly-commuting distance from your garden.

During the last decade wildlife has increasingly moved into towns, with only those forms that have been able to adapt to the new environment surviving. If we are to be successful in giving nature a helping hand then it will probably be the result of the cumulative efforts of individuals through their gardens. You can aid nature by buying the pupae or chrysalides of many species of butterflies from butterfly farms. Butterflies eat green material only during the larval stage, the adult insect takes nectar throughout its life and will fly to such flowers as scabious, candytuft, sedum and buddleia, whilst the last of the Red Admirals and Peacocks will feed upon Michaelmas daisies and the juice of fallen fruit, before taken their final meal from ivy in October and hibernating for the winter. All of these flowers are a pleasure in themselves, worthy of inclusion in any plan, and by simply remembering them you can be sure of the constant presence of the brightest butterflies during the late summer days, when they are on the wing.

Insects are often thought of as being the enemy of the gardener, but this is an inaccurate and unfair accusation. Admittedly there are pests such as the Cabbage White butterflies (both large and small), and the onion and carrot root flies, which exploit our crops, but they are very much in the minority and for every vegetarian pest there is usually a specialist predator that will provide natural protection. Moreover, insects are essential for the pollination of plants, and without them performing that role we would be incapable of providing even the most basic of foods. Gardeners can do a great deal to protect this important natural resource, by selecting a small number of subjects, perhaps only one or two, such as buddleia and honeysuckle, which will attract the widest range of nectar-feeding insects.

Water gardens are a natural home for frogs and toads, and if you have a pond or part of a pond that is fish-free (the fish would eat the eggs and tadpoles), look out for the spawn appearing during late March and early April. Frogs tend to return to the area in which they were raised to spawn and can now be found in town centres. Acquire some spawn or tadpoles in the spring – seek a man-made site, *never* raid a natural habitat – and place them in your pond. If the pond has had the opportunity to establish itself, it will already be supporting sufficient life to feed the amphibians and you will not need to supplement their diet. In August the lily pads will become covered in tiny black jumping objects, and the tadpoles will have metamorphosed into frogs. No longer dependent upon the pond, they will move around the garden feeding on insects and all manner of garden pests, asking no more from their human hosts than the provision of some loose stones under which to hibernate, so that they may emerge again in the spring to start the whole process over again.

Loose stones, dense growth and similar areas that provide cover and protection are the prerequisites of keeping wildlife in the garden. Hedgehogs and slow worms, that seek the warmth of the compost heap, and sun-basking lizards may all find their way into your garden and rear their young if you provide them with the necessary shelter. No odd corner is too remote, nor few geographical situations too removed from the countryside to attract a whole range of wildlife. In the past the gardener has turned to insecticides to kill his foes in the garden, but the chemical that destroys the aphids will also destroy the ladybirds that prey on them and keep the pest problems to manageable proportions. When the aphids return, as they inevitably do, there are no predators and the problem becomes greater, reaching epidemic proportions. More insecticides are then required until it all becomes some dreadful horticultural addiction. Insecticides *have* been developed that are specific for certain pests, but today we live in a more enlightened age, and we know that if we upset the balance of nature (albeit in a way that we think we have under control), the unpredictable effects will sooner or later become

apparent. Increasing numbers of people are dealing with the pest problem by living at peace with nature and attracting the widest possible range of wildlife into the garden. The natural balance that results means that only a very small part of the plant kingdom suffers from the actions of the original predators.

Very little effort is required to attract birds into the garden, especially the robin, who so faithfully follows our efforts at digging in winter and spring, and the blackbird. Each bird has its own carefully marked-out territory. A policy of attracting insects into the garden will bring with it insectivorous birds such as tits and summer visitors such as martins. Seed-eaters may be attracted by cotoneasters which will provide bright berries during the winter months before the birds take their final feed, and if you provide cover the thrush will keep a constant vigil against slugs and snails. In addition to the natural methods, a feeding table can be placed near to the focal point from the main window, and if it is charged with seeds, dunnocks, finches and tits will come to feed regularly providing constant movement. The smaller birds will wait on the fence for the larger and more aggressive birds to take their fill before arriving at the table. Nature knows no boundary, and different species, particularly during a cold spell, will fly into the table. Those people who live by a wood, or where a wood has recently been felled to make way for houses, may find woodpeckers coming into the garden, or even a squirrel. In the short dark days of winter the garden is as alive as at any time of the year, and the contented gardener may gaze out at the wonders of nature, but only if he has landscaped his garden and designed it with that in mind.

III PLANTS FOR ALL LANDSCAPES

(These lists, which are by no means exhaustive, cover the more popular plants, all of which are easily grown and are ideally suited to the small urban garden. Many of the names refer to either genuses or species, and where these occur it may be assumed that all or most are suited to the purpose.)

Subjects for Prolonged Colour in Alpine Gardens

Alyssum (white and mauve)
Arabis
Aricula
Campanula
Cheiranthus
Crane's bill (Geranium)
Crocus
Cyclamen (C. neapolitanum)
Daffodil (miniature)
Dianthus
Gentiana
Geum
Helianthemum
Iris (dwarf species)
Muscari
Ranunculus
Rhododendron (dwarf species)
Saxifraga
Sedum
Sempervivum
Thyme
Tulip

Dwarf Conifers for the Rock Garden

Chamaecyparis obtusa
Juniperus horizontalis
Picea abies
Pinus sylvestris Beuvronensis

Hedging Plants for Urban Gardens

Beech
Berberis
Box
Camellia
Chamaecyparis (C. lawsonia – Lawson Cypress)
Chaenomeles (Moules japonica)
Cupressocyparis (C. leylandii – Leyland Cypress)
Cupressus (C. macrocarpa – Monterey Cypress)
Escallonia
Forsythia
Hawthorn
Holly
Hornbeam
Lavender
Rose
Rosmarinus officinalis (Rosemary)
Veronica
Yew

Easy-to-Grow Trees and Shrubs for Small Gardens

Acer palmatum
Azalea
Birch
Box
Broom
Chaenomeles (Moules japonica)
Cistus
Cotoneaster
Daphne
Escallonia
Forsythia
Fuchsia
Hebe
Holly
Hydrangea
Jasmine
Laburnum
Lavender
Magnolia
Mahonia
Malus (Apple)
Potentilla
Prunus (Cherry, Plum and Almond)
Rhus (especially R. typhina, or Sumach)
Rose
Skimmia japonica
Spiraea
Viburnum

Fig 87 Dramatic in its form, the flowering prunus lights up both the garden and the street scene.

Plants for Shady Positions

Trees and Shrubs

Azalea
Berberis
Camellia
Chaenomeles (Moules japonica)
Cotoneaster
Forsythia
Hedera
Hydrangea
Ligustrum
Mahonia
Rhododendron (dwarf species)
Ribes (especially American Currant)
Skimmia japonica
Viburnum

Perennials

Anemone japonica
Aquilegia
Astilbe
Cowslip (Primula veris)
Helleborus
Hosta
Polyanthus
Primrose
Primula
Trollius

Plants that are Easy to Grow on Chalky (Lime) Soils

Aconitum
Allium
Anemone japonica
Aquilega
Arabis
Artemisia

Fig 88 Use can be made of the shaded areas under trees by planting bulbs for 'naturalising'. They welcome the spring and will have completed their flowering before the leaves appear on the trees in May.

Aster
Astilbe
Aubrieta
Berberis
Birch
Box
Buddleia
Campanula
Chaenomeles (Moules japonica)
Cheiranthus (Siberian Wallflower)
Chrysanthemum
Clarkia
Clematis
Cotoneaster
Crocus
Cyclamen neapolitanum
Cypress (Lawson)
Cypress (Leyland)
Daffodil
Dahlia
Dianthus
Elder
Escallonia
Euphorbia
Forsythia
Fritillary
Fuchsia
Geranium
Gladiolus
Godetia
Gypsophila
Helichrysum
Helleborus
Hibiscus
Hosta
Holly
Hyacinth
Iris
Laburnum
Lavender
Lilies (various)
Lobelia
Lupin
Mahonia
Malus (Apple)
Muscari

Narcissus
Paeony
Pansy
Petunia
Phlox
Potentilla
Prunus (Cherry, Plum and Almond)
Pyrethrum
Ribes (American Currant)
Rhus
Rose
Rosemary
Ranunculus
Salvia
Saxifraga
Scabious
Sedum
Sempervivum
Thyme
Trollius
Veronica
Viburnum
Wisteria
Yew
Zinnia

Gold and Purple Plants

Many of the yellow- and gold-leaved plants are sports of the commoner green forms. So that you can identify foliage plants which possess leaves of a gold or yellow shade, the name of the familiar plant will have the suffix 'Aurea' or 'Aureus' (derived from the Latin *aurus*, meaning gold) added. Thus you will see *Erica carnea* 'Aurea', a yellow heather, and *Humulus lupulus* 'Aureus', the golden hop. Others will possess English variety names from which it will be obvious that a gold or yellow is involved, as in Golden Ivy – *Hedera helix* 'Buttercup' – or the golden *Cupressus macrocarpa* 'Goldcrest'.

The other common mutant forms of foliage is that of the red-brown or purple shades. Most plants displaying this sport will be identified by 'Purpureum', 'Atropurpureum' or 'Purpurea' in their name. Particularly useful for providing purple colour in the garden are maples, particularly *Acer palmatum* 'Atropurpureum', *Malus* (Apple) and *Berberis*.

The cultivation of these sports is similar to that of the dominant green form, so you should consult a plantsmen's catalogue, seek out the yellow-gold or purple forms, and then check which plant they are derived from.

Plants of Medium Height for Colour or Dramatic Form

Delphiniums
Flag Lilies
Foxgloves
Hollyhocks
Lupins
Pampas Grass
Red Hot Poker

Plants with Perfumed Flowers or Leaves

American Currant
Buddleia
Hyacinth
Jasmine
Lavender
Lemon Balm
Lilac
Lily of the Valley
Mimosa
Mint
Mock Orange (*Philadelphus coronarius*)
Myrtle
Nicotiana
Pink (*Dianthus*)
Rosemary
Siberian Wallflower (*Cheiranthus allionii*)
Skimmia japonica
Thyme
Viburnum fragrans
Wallflower
Wisteria

Climbing Plants for the Small Garden

Clematis
Cotoneaster
Hydrangea petiolaris
Ivy
Pyracantha
Passion Flower (*Passiflora*)
Roses (various)
Virginia Creeper
Wisteria

Plants that Must Have Acid Soils

Azalea
Calluna
Camellia
Erica
Gentian
Magnolia
Pieris
Rhododendron

Dwarf Conifers Suitable for Small Layouts

Chamaecyparis lawsoniana 'Minima'

Fig 89 Azaleas greet the spring with a whole range of colours at the red end of the spectrum.

Chamaecyparis lawsoniana 'Nana'
Juniperus horizontalis
Juniperus procumbens 'Nana'
Picea abies 'Nidiformis'
Pinus sylvestris Beuvronensis

Cottage Garden Plants

Black-eyed Susan (*Thunbergia alata*)
Bleeding Heart (*Dicentra spectabilis*)
Bluebell
Buddleia (especially *B. davidii* var. and *B. globosa*)
Burning Bush
Californian Poppy
Candytuft
Canterbury Bells (*Campanula medium*)
Cornflower (*Centaurea cyanus*)
Cowslip (*Primula veris*)
Crown Imperial (*Fritillaria imperialis*)
Cyclamen
Flag Lily (Bearded Iris)
Forget-me-not (*Myosotis*)
Foxglove (*Digitalis*)
Fritillary (*Fritillaria meleagris*)

Golden Rod (*Solidago*)
Hollyhocks
Honesty (*Lunaria annua*)
Honeysuckle (*Lonicera*)
Jasmine
Larkspur
Lenten Rose (*Helleborus orientalis*)
Lilac
London Pride
Love-in-a-mist (*Nigella damascena*)
Love-lies-Bleeding (*Amaranthus caudatus*)
Lupin
Madonna Lily (*Lilium candidum*)
Marguerite
Marigold (both *Calendula* and *Tagetes*)
Michaelmas Daisy (*Aster novi-belgii*)
Mignonette (*Reseda odorata*)
Periwinkle (*Vinca* species)
Scabious
Sea Campion (*Silene vulgaris maritima*)
Sea Holly (*Eryngium maritimum*)
Snapdragon (*Antirrhinum majus*)
Snowdrop
Solomon's Seal (*Polygonatum*)
Sweet Pea (*Lathyrus odoratus*)
Sweet William (*Dianthus barbatus*)
Tobacco Plant (*Nicotiana tabacum*)
Traveller's Joy (*Clematis vitalba*)
Tulip
Violet
Winter Aconite (*Eranthis hyemalis*)
Wolf's Bane (*Aconitum vulparia*)

Plants for Exposed Sites

Anemone japonica
Berberis darwinii
Berberis thunbergii
Calluna
Chaenomeles (*Moules japonica*)
Cotoneaster
Erica
Fuchsia magellanica
Holly
Ivy
Jasminum nudiflorum (Winter Jasmine)

Fig 90 Spring borders should be planted for brightness, to cheer up the days which are still dull. The red of the daisy picks out the stripe in the tulip, while the white lightens the whole effect and blends in with everything.

Fig 91 The humble marigold provides just the correct degree of colour growing in this paved area.

Juniper
Lavender
Mahonia
Malus species
Pieris japonica
Privet
Prunus (Cherry and Almond)
Rhododendron
Ribes (Currant)
Thyme
Viburnum
Willow
Yew

Plants for Patios, Tubs, Window Boxes and Hanging Baskets

Summer

Ageratum
Antirrhinum
Begonia (Fibrous- and tuberous-rooted)

Fuchsia
Impatiens walleriana (Busy Lizzie)
Lobelia
Nemisia
Petunia
Rose (miniature)
Salvia
Tagetes

Spring

Aubrieta
Daffodil species
Hyacinth
Muscari (Grape Hyacinth)
Narcissus species
Tulip species
Wallflower

Index

price
£6.49

what's inside

Check out some of the cool things inside!

Daisy and Digger P110

P42 Quiz

P86 Hairstyles

honey b

ISBN 0-85116-840-X

Dolphins
P58

Snoop's Story
P90

P16
Poppy's
Party
Guide

P24
All
About
Me...

DOMiNO
P6

P98
Big Cats

DoMiNo

Normally Annie's family loves having visitors...

But this was one letter that I knew smelled of trouble –

Just then, Annie appeared —

What's that, Domino? Oh, it's a letter for Mum.

Uh-oh! I recognise that handwriting!

So did I! Cats have good memories.

Annie took the letter to Mum.

Not another bill, Annie.

No, Mum. It's worse! It's from Great Aunt Betty!

10

COOL GIR

Woof!
I'm Clifford and my owner is Candie. Wanna know all about us and our friends, the Cool Girls? Get reading!

ALL ABOUT ME...

full name: Sir Clifford Cool Dog of Bark-shire
likes: cuddles from Candie, walks, playing with my toys, dog treats, leaving a trail of muddy pawprints
dislikes: having a bath
favourite colour: chocolate brown, like my lovely fur
fave food: roast beef - mmm!
most favourite thing: Candie!

CANDIE COOL GIRL

Candie is the leader of the Cool Girls. I go everywhere with her - she never leaves me out. Candie is sporty and fun and likes to play games. She loves to go out on her scooter or skates with Poppy. I get lots of exercise running after them. Candie hates being bored!

fave food: stringy spaghetti
fave colour: blue
ideal pet: me, of course!

FI-FI FASHION GIRL

Fi-Fi comes from France and loves all things fashion. She's always trying out the latest looks. She loves chocolates. Her favourite things are shoes, handbags and hair accessories. Fi-Fi always carries her mirror! She hates anything messy - especially outdoor sports.

fave food: chocolate cake
fave colour: lilac
ideal pet: a stylish miniature French poodle. Fi-Fi would buy her the glitziest collars and they could wear matching hair ribbons.

POPPY PARTY GIRL

Poppy just loves to party! She loves singing, dancing and acting. She takes her personal CD player everywhere. Poppy is always thinking of fab party ideas for her Cool Girl pals - the more glittery and sparkly, the better. Her very best friend is Fi-Fi. Poppy really dislikes having to sit still for more than 5 minutes.

fave food: party nibbles
fave colour: super shiny silver
ideal pet: Poppy's always jumping around, so what could be better than a boingy kangaroo?

14

SUZI SHOPPING GIRL

Suzi is a shopping queen. There can never be too many shops! She's always out with Fi-Fi helping her choose outfits and accessories. She gets all the best bargains. If the Cool Girls need something, Suzi knows just where to go. She hates having sore feet and sleeping - the only things that stop her shopping!

fave food: any fast food - more time for shopping!
fave colour: red
ideal pet: Suzi needs a sweet little pony and cart to help her carry home all her purchases.

CAT CHATTY GIRL

Cat loves to chat all day long. She's always on the phone, on her mobile or emailing her friends. When she starts talking, she never stops! Cat's also a gadget girl - she loves to get the latest games and new stuff for her computer. She hates being quiet and it'd be a huge disaster if she ever lost her mobile.

fave food: pizza
fave colour: yellow
ideal pets: a cute kitty for Cat *and* a chit-chatty parrot!

Poppy's

Hi girls, I'm Poppy Cool Girl and I just love to party. I've got lotsa great ideas for an animal-tastic sleepover party.

who to invite

Three or four of your best mates. If it's too crowded, your sleepover won't be much fun.

please come to my animal sleepover at

on

Make these sweet kitty invites - they're easy to do. You'll need coloured card, coloured pens and some stick-on wiggle eyes (get these from craft shops).

All you have to do is cut the card into invite sized pieces, copy out this cute design and then stick on the wobbly eyes. Write on the details of your party and that's it. Mix the colours of card and pens to make each invite different.

what to wear

Animal pics and patterns are everywhere on cute tops, t-shirts, pjs, accessories and bags.

Ask all your guests to wear something with an animal motif.

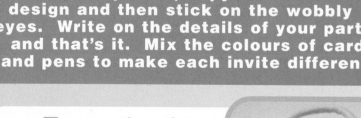

party guide

what to do

Sleepovers are perfect for watching fun films, so get a video or two. Here are my top 5 furry faves –

101 Dalmatians
My Dog Skip
Far From Home
Beethoven
Jungle Book

what to scoff

Anything animal shaped. Use an animal cookie cutter to make special sandwiches or make your own mini pizzas. Mix up a pack of pizza base dough, roll it out and cut into animal shapes. Now add your fave pizza toppings and bake.

Gummi Bears, chewy jelly hippos, jelly snakes and foam shrimps are perfect for munching. If you're having cake, choose one shaped like a cute animal. Lots of supermarkets stock them.

Here's a delish smoothie recipe for you to try -

jungle juice

Whisk together a carton of pineapple juice and a can of coconut milk. Put some ice cubes into glasses and pour out the smoothie mix. Cut up chunks of banana, apple, orange, strawberry and pineapple and push on to bright straws to decorate. Mmm!

party bags

If you're giving your guests a party bag to take home, here are some cool ideas for things to put in them –

animal roller stamper
cute erasers
animal stickers
butterfly hair clips
anything from Hello Kitty

* Remember to always ask an adult before using any kitchen equipment.

lend ANIMAL CHARITIES

There are loads of brilliant animal charities who are all dedicated to helping animals. Charities like WWF, Born Free, Care For The Wild and WDCS are all working to try to stop cruelty to animals and prevent them suffering. These charities want to teach people to treat animals with respect.

BE A SUPPORTER

Animal charities rely on people to support them so that they can continue to help animals across the world. There are a few ways of helping them but the most fun is probably adopting one of the animals the charities have rescued and rehomed.

a Paw!

BORN FREE

You can adopt a gorgeous tiger called Roque. He was rescued from a Spanish pet shop window. He had only been a few days old when he was taken from his mother and put on sale. Born Free rescued the young cub and he now lives in a large forest enclosure at Born Free's tiger sanctuary in India.

BORN FREE FOUNDATION

When you adopt him you'll be sent a special adoption certificate telling you all about Roque, a full colour photograph, regular updates about how he is getting on, a folder and stickers.

To find out more ask an adult if you can log on to www.bornfree.org.uk or write to 'Born Free, 3 Grove House, Foundry Lane, Horsham, West Sussex, RH13 5PL.

19

CARE FOR THE WILD

Little Natumi was rescued when her herd strayed onto a human settlement and her mum was tragically killed. Natumi was taken to a nursery in Nairobi, Africa, where she received lots of loving care from the keepers. When she was one year old she was taken to Kenya's Tsavo East National Park where she now lives with lots of other orphaned elephants.

You will receive an adoption certificate with a colour picture of little Natumi, a cool story book, a window sticker and regular updates from Kenya to tell you how she is doing.

To find out more write to Care For The Wild, The Granary, Tickford Farm, Kinsfold, West Sussex, RH12 3SE or ask an adult if you can log on to their website – www.careforthewild.com

WWF

Zhu Xiong was rescued by WWF when she was found in a village causing chaos. She was very confused and frightened. She was taken to the Wanglang Reserve in China where she will live with another 30 pandas in the reserve.

WDCS

Lightning is one of the many dolphins that WDCS look after in the Moray Firth, Scotland. He is a very energetic young dolphin and is a super-fast swimmer. Money raised by adopting a dolphin with WDCS helps them protect dolphins around the world.

When you adopt Lightning by Direct Debit, you will receive a video, an adoption certificate, a picture of Lightning with lots of information about him, a magazine, newsletters throughout the year and a window sticker.

WDCS
Whale and Dolphin Conservation Society

To find out more ask an adult to log on to www.wdcs.org or write to them at WDCS, Brookfield House, 38 St Paul Street, Chippenham, Wiltshire, SN15 1LY.

WWF

If you adopt Zhu Xiong you will receive a certificate, a colour photograph of her and regular updates on how she's doing throughout the year.

If you'd like more information about how to adopt her then ask an adult if you can log on to www.wwf.org.uk or write to WWF, Panda House, Weyside Park, Godalming, Surrey, GU7 1XR.

monkey

Don't let these chimps make a chump out of you!

GOING APE!

These words all end in APE. Can you guess what they are from the clues?

Type of cloak _ APE

A fruit _ _ APE

Part of the neck _ APE

To mould _ _ APE

A joke _ APE

To get away _ _ _ APE

NAME GAME

Cross out the letters that appear more than once in these squares to find out three chimps' names.

B	F	E
A	S	B
E	Y	S

F	U	B
S	E	S
N	U	F

S	Y	B
Y	A	U
A	B	E

WAY TO GO!

Which vine will take Mo and Molly to the Tree Top Cafe?

A   B   C

CAFE

22

business

SPOT THE DIFFERENCE

Chester and Charlie are twins, but they're not identical. Can you spot 4 differences between them?

MONKEY NUTS

Put these nuts in the correct place on the grid and a chimp's fave food will appear in the shaded area.

PEANUT   ALMOND   BRAZIL
PECAN   WALNUT   HAZELNUT

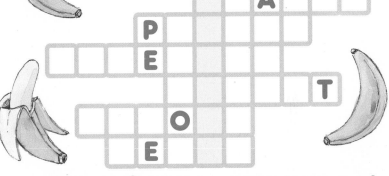

MONKEY SEARCH

Can you find all these monkeys and apes in the wordsearch? They can be found reading up, down, backwards, forwards and diagonally.

CHIMPANZEE   GORILLA   ORANGUTAN
SPIDER   BABOON   MONKEY   APE   TAMARIN
RHESUS   HOWLER   MARMOSET   BARBARY

C	H	I	M	P	A	N	Z	E	E
B	N	D	A	I	M	P	O	O	N
A	A	E	R	E	O	I	E	R	I
R	T	B	M	L	Y	D	I	H	R
B	U	S	O	W	E	H	L	E	A
A	G	P	S	O	K	O	L	S	M
R	N	I	E	H	N	W	A	U	A
Y	A	D	T	M	O	N	Z	S	T
O	R	E	A	H	M	A	R	M	O
G	O	R	I	L	L	A	M	A	R

23

ALL ABOUT ME

Hi! My name's Marisa and I live with my mum, dad and big sister, Kelsey.

I love animals but Kelsey prefers Gareth Gates.

My fave times are when we visit Auntie Susan on her farm. First I play with Tiger the cat then Auntie Susan tells me that Hattie Hare has a surprise for me.

She's had babies! They're gorgeous! There are 4 brown and 2 black ones.

I get to hold one very gently — aww!

Next I have fun with Skye the dog then it's time to start work.

It's my job to collect the eggs that the hens have laid.

Auntie Susan has all sorts of hens and chicks. These ones are called Silkies.

Kelsey helps me feed the hens but we leave the turkeys to Auntie Susan — they're scary.

Now the horses need grooming. Poppy the pony's just the right size for me.

Then Auntie Susan lets me ride Poppy. Cool!

I feed Tam a few carrots then it's almost time to leave.

Indoors, what a surprise! Donald the duck's swimming in the bath! Skye's surprised too! Auntie Susan tells us that Donald had a problem with the waterproofing on his feathers so they're testing it out.

What a fab day! Kelsey and me sit on Tam's cart and pretend we're going to travel home in style — by pony and trap!

Wildlife

giant pandas

They are called Xiongmao in Chinese, which means Giant Cat Bear, but we know them better as Giant Pandas. Find out more about these lovable bears from China.

HOW DO I LOOK?

* Their fur colour is white with black eye patches, ears, legs, feet, chest and shoulders.

* The fur is thick and coarse and slightly oily to stop water getting through to their skin.

* An adult male is 1.2m - 1.7m tall, weighs between 100 - 150kgms and can live for up to 25 years.

* Their heads are very large and their tails are very short.

* Pandas have an extra finger to help them grip bamboo stalks.

* They cannot walk on their hind legs and prefer to sit down while eating.

WHERE CAN YOU FIND ME?

* Pandas can only be found living in the wild in central China.

* They live in the damp, misty bamboo forests, high in the mountains.

* Although it is very cold in winter, unlike other bears, pandas do not hibernate.

* They prefer to live alone.

PANDA NOSH

Pandas' favourite food is bamboo, bamboo and more bamboo! They will occasionally eat a small rodent or fish, but this is very rare. However, like other bears, they have a very sweet tooth and have been known to break into farmers' beehives to get the honey!

CUTE CUBS

* Panda mums give birth once a year and usually have 1 - 2 babies.

* They are born in August or September, in a hollow tree or cave.

* The babies are called cubs.

* They are tiny, just 15cm long and weigh 100 gms.

* The babies are blind, hairless and all white.

* After a month, the black spots begin to appear.

* By 5 months of age they are walking, running and playing.

* At 6 - 9 months, they begin eating bamboo.

* Cubs stay with their mums until they are 18 months old.

PANDA PATTER

Pandas are quite vocal and have up to eleven different calls, which include bleats, honks, squeals, groans, moans and even barks!

DID YOU KNOW?

* People in the Western World only found out about Giant Pandas in 1869 when a French missionary discovered them.

* They are probably the most endangered species with less than 1000 Giant Pandas alive in the wild.

* The panda is the symbol of peace in China.

A DAY IN THE LIFE...

Pandas spend two-thirds of their day eating and the rest of the day resting! They need to eat lots and lots of bamboo to survive and have very strong teeth to crunch through the bamboo stalks. They move around very slowly and have no place they call home. They just sleep where they happen to be at the time they feel sleepy!

PANDA PERIL

Pandas are under threat from poachers and the destruction by man of the bamboo forests, where they live and eat. To find out how to help or adopt a panda, turn to pages 18 - 21.

31

WHAT'S YOUR STYLE?

Are you like a pampered panda or are you more a sporty zebra or jewellery-mad jackdaw? Follow this flowchart to find out - the answer's there in black and white!

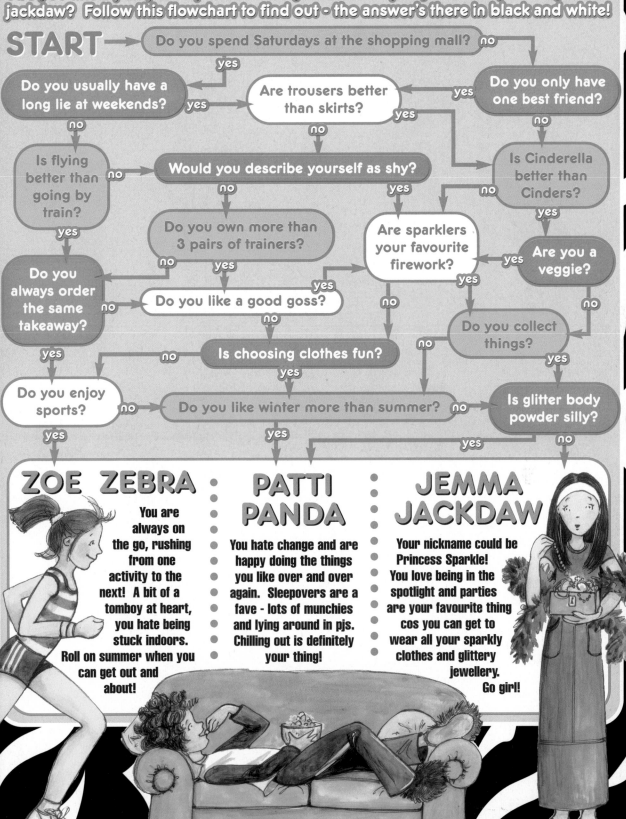

START → Do you spend Saturdays at the shopping mall? — **no**

yes

Do you usually have a long lie at weekends? — **yes** → Are trousers better than skirts? ← **yes** — Do you only have one best friend?

no — **yes** — **no**

Is flying better than going by train? ← **no** — Would you describe yourself as shy? → Is Cinderella better than Cinders?

yes — **no** — **yes** — **no** — **yes**

Do you always order the same takeaway? ← **no** — Do you own more than 3 pairs of trainers? — Are sparklers your favourite firework? ← **yes** — Are you a veggie?

no — **yes** — **yes** — **no**

yes — Do you like a good goss? — **yes** — Do you collect things? — **no**

no — **no** — **yes**

Is choosing clothes fun? — **no**

yes

Do you enjoy sports? ← **no** — Do you like winter more than summer? — **no** → Is glitter body powder silly?

yes — **yes** — **yes** — **no**

ZOE ZEBRA
You are always on the go, rushing from one activity to the next! A bit of a tomboy at heart, you hate being stuck indoors. Roll on summer when you can get out and about!

PATTI PANDA
You hate change and are happy doing the things you like over and over again. Sleepovers are a fave - lots of munchies and lying around in pjs. Chilling out is definitely your thing!

JEMMA JACKDAW
Your nickname could be Princess Sparkle! You love being in the spotlight and parties are your favourite thing cos you can get to wear all your sparkly clothes and glittery jewellery.
Go girl!

Wendy

I love it here — it's so peaceful.

Wendy Thornley's dad owns Rose Lodge Riding School and Stables. Wendy loves horses and has two of her own, Penny and Miss Dixie. One morning, by the beach . . .

A horse! Where did he come from? He's a beauty.

I've never seen him before. He's not one of Dad's.

Whoa, boy! Come here.

Wendy! Wendy, come on. It's time to get up.

Mmm? What?

It was all a dream! The horse seemed so real!

At the stables, Wendy met one of the instructors.

I hope you haven't forgotten about the picnic ride tomorrow.

Of course not, Mark. What's the weather going to be like?

The forecast is good.

Great! I love picnic rides in summer.

Wendy took Dixie for a ride.

Let's go a different way today, girl. We'll head for the beach.

35

Nearly there, Dixie. Wow! This is the meadow I saw in my dream!

Then —

This is spooky. There's a horse exactly like the one in my dream.

Wendy tried to catch the frightened horse, but —

This is no use. He won't let Dixie come close. I'll need help.

Back at Rose Lodge, Wendy phoned the police.

Has anyone reported a missing horse today?

Yes. A chestnut stallion escaped from the Thomsons' farm earlier, Wendy.

I saw him in the meadow behind the old windmill.

I'll tell Mr Thomson to get over there. D'you think your father would help catch it?

So —

John, can you get Mark and come and help me?

Of course, Mr Thornley.

36

Back at the meadow —

If we all approach from different directions, we should be able to catch him.

Sure enough —

Got you! Easy, boy — easy.

Just then, the owner turned up.

I'm very grateful to you all. Sovereign is a valuable horse.

My dream had a happy ending!

Early next morning —

Here are the first riders for the picnic ride.

Their ponies are ready.

Hi, Wendy. Which ponies are we riding?

You've got first pick, Sammy!

The last rider to arrive was Ellen Drew.

Where are your riding gloves, Ellen?

In my pocket. Don't fuss, Dad.

Before the ride left —

There are three back packs for the food, first aid kit and rainwear.

First aid? Are you expecting accidents?

No, but my riders always go prepared, Mrs Drew.

37

Mark led the way. Some time later —

We'll be stopping soon for lunch. Meanwhile, keep your eyes open. There's a lot of wildlife around here.

Look! There's a fox over there.

Wow! I've never seen one this close before.

This looks like a good place to have our picnic.

Thank goodness. I'm starving!

First things first. Unsaddle your ponies and let them have a drink in the lake.

When they've had a drink, tie them up in the shade.

There you are, Penny. Isn't that nice?

Are you enjoying yourself, Wendy?

Yes, it's lovely out here.

Suddenly —

Oops! My sandwich paper!

I'll get it.

The wind is getting stronger.

Let's finish our picnic before it gets too windy.

Then —

I don't like the look of those clouds.

As the riders set off again —

The rain's going to pour.

Take shelter while I get the rain capes out.

I hope it doesn't get much worse. We're a long way from Rose Lodge.

Continued on page 78

39

rescued!

This is Pip. He's a miniature Shetland Pony, but what makes him even more special is the fact that he is only just 27 inches high (68cm).

Some people breed miniature horses to be even smaller than they should be, which is on average 40 inches (101 cm). But some of the tiny animals are born with incredibly short legs and are seen as having no use so they are put to sleep. This was what lay in store for poor Pip until he was taken to Wellington Farm Rescue Centre in Devon where he now lives happily with the other rescued horses there.

His best friend is Trojan, a Shire horse who was also rescued and taken to live on the farm. Trojan was the first horse to arrive at the centre. He'd had a terrible start in life. When he was only 10 months old his owners found out that he was only a $\frac{3}{4}$ shire horse, and not a full shire. They were very disappointed and as a result they underfed and mistreated him. Luckily a lady heard about his bad treatment and offered to buy him.

However, when Trojan became too big for her to handle, he was brought to the centre where he is now a huge 9 year old gentle giant.

Pip and Trojan have a very happy life together at the centre and love playing with each other.

Pip is now starring in his very own set of books written by Allan Candy. They are based on Pip's real life adventures and all the characters on the farm.

To find out more about the books and where you can get your hands on a copy ask an adult to log on to www.ponyrescue.org. Money made from the book will help to feed and look after all the animals at Wellington Farm Rescue Centre.

want to work

There are loads of jobs where you can work with animals, but which one would you be most suited to? Try our quiz to find out.

1. At school you look forward to lessons in...
a. science and biology.
c. art and craft.
b. P.E.

2. In your spare time you can be found...
c. with a pair of scissors in your hand ready to make something.
b. playing with your pets or your friends' pets.
a. down at your local animal centre helping out.

3. What's your fave animal?
a. You love them all from snakes to kittens.
b. Dogs and puppies.
c. Anything cute and fluffy with lots of fur.

4. You've got loads of homework to do. Do you...
b. put it off for as long as possible then get it done.
a. get stuck in. You don't actually mind doing it.
c. spend ages doodling on the pages before you get the homework done.

5. Your friend cuts her finger and there's blood everywhere. How do you react?
a. You know exactly what to do and don't panic.
c. You hate the sight of blood and have to leave before you faint.
b. You're not too keen to look, but do your best to help your friend.

6. Your favourite holiday destination would be...
b. anywhere where there's lots to do. You like to keep busy.
c. a girlie holiday with lots of pampering and treats.
a. an African safari so you could see all the wild animals close up.

42

Mostly a

You would make a great vet. You love animals and helping them. Being a vet takes a long time and you need to do well at school so keep the brain cells working! The best thing to do would be get as much experience with animals as you can. Ask a parent if you can help out at a local shelter – good luck!

Mostly b

You'd make a great puppy trainer for the Guide Dogs' Association. You need to be prepared to do a lot of walking with the dogs, sometimes a trainer will walk miles and miles in a day. You also need to have a lot of patience to train the dogs. You'll need lots of experience with animals so ask an adult if you can help out at a local kennels.

Mostly c

Dog grooming would be a great job for you as you love to be creative. It's not all cutting cute dogs' hair, though, as you've got to learn yukky stuff about little flees and lice that live on dogs too! There are loads of courses that you can go on to learn how to become a first class groomer.

PUPPY

Hi girls, Candie Cool Girl here. Me 'n' Clifford have lots of puppy care tips for you.

your puppy is ...

... 8 weeks old

and has probably just left its mum, brothers and sisters so let it run around, sniff and explore. It'll need 4 small meals a day, but maybe won't eat much for the first day or so until it gets used to its new home.

Use the puppy's name every time you speak to it and praise it when it pays attention. If your pup is lonely and cries at night don't be tempted to let it into your room. Try leaving a radio on low to comfort it instead.

Start house training straight away by taking your puppy out in the morning, after meals, when it wakes up and before bed. Always use the same command such as 'busy' or 'be clean'. Give it lots of praise each time it goes to the loo. Remember that puppies need to go a lot and excitement can make them worse, so don't be cross if there are any little accidents!

BEFORE YOUR PUPPY ARRIVES YOU'LL NEED TO GET

A BED - use a cardboard box lined with a cosy blanket while your puppy is small. As it grows, just get a bigger box. When it's older, a hard plastic dog bed with a comfy liner will be easy to keep clean – and hard to chew!

2 BOWLS - one for food and one for water.

PUPPY FOOD - ask the owner what your puppy has been eating as a change of food can be upsetting.

TOYS - puppies love to play. But make sure toys are safe and can't be easily destroyed by sharp puppy teeth.

A COLLAR AND LEAD - don't forget the ID disc.

A NAME - choose one that's short and easy for your puppy to learn.

Power

... 12 weeks old

and should have had all its vaccinations by now. Wait for 10 - 14 days after the last jab before taking your pup to public places. It should now know its name and simple commands such as 'no' and 'sit'.

The commands 'come' and 'stay' are very important so teach these as soon as poss. They can stop your pup from getting into dangerous situations.

Come - to call your pup say its name and then 'come'. Make it sound really exciting. When your puppy gets it right give it a treat and lots of praise. Make it into a game by throwing toys and then calling your pup back.

Stay - ask your pup to sit, then with the palm of your hand facing it, tell it to stay while you move away a little. Now move back towards your pup and praise it. Move further away each time you practise.

Remember ...

... to keep training sessions short and make them fun.

... finish when your pup has done a good thing so that it enjoys the lessons.

... not to shout at naughty puppies. A deep, firm tone will soon let it know who's boss.

... if you need more help your vet will have info on local training and obedience classes.

Bonjour, mes petites. Think you have nothing to wear? Well, you can get lots of looks with one pair of jeans. Good, non?

gotta have it!

And I've picked out the sweetest accessories to finish off your outfits.

Choose a dark shade of jeans because they can look smarter than paler ones. Bootcut styles look good with heels or flat shoes.

46

summer

Perfect for meeting your friends in the park, holiday sight-seeing or sunny afternoon barbeques.

add ...

vest tops
pretty belts
flower accessories
canvas trainers

summer essential - fruity lip balm

groovy

Cool for a beach cover-up or summer evenings in the garden.

add ...

gypsy tops
sparkly flip-flops

beaded belts
butterfly and flower accessories

groovy essential - funky sunglasses

smart

You can wear jeans to family gatherings and outings.

add ...

shirt
fitted jacket
matching shoes
and bag
simple chain
necklace

smart essential - neat hair, so splash out on cool clips

cute

The sweetest shopping outfit.

cute essential - shiny lip gloss

add ... sandals
sparkly hair clips or bobbles
sugar candy colours
sweet t-shirt tops

sporty

Cute and casual for a mate's sleepover party or perfect for a fun park visit.

add ...

slogan tops
hoodies
matching trainers
studded belts

sporty essential - funky backpack

disco

disco essential - body glitter

add ...

silky or shimmery tops
strappy sandals
mini clubbing bag
matching jewellery

bling, bling, baby!

Get instant bling with this fab Sparkle Spray from Tulip. Just spray it on to your denim, shine like a star and then wash it off again. Cool! Sparkle Spray comes in silver, gold and irridescent, costs £5.99 and is available from craft and fabric shops.

DoMiNo

Continued from page 11

Continued from page 11

Annie's great Auntie Betty had come to stay and she was hard work!

Thank goodness I managed to smuggle you up here without Auntie Betty seeing, Domino.

There's no way she'd let you in my bedroom!

Later —

Mum, why are you vacuuming in here again?

Auntie Betty keeps complaining about cat hairs.

But the place is practically spotless!

I know, Annie, but it's better to keep her happy.

Why don't you just stand up to her? It's your house.

I just want a quiet life.

And, anyway, her bark's worse than her bite.

Tell that to Domino. She'd rather face a Doberman than Auntie Betty.

It was true! With Auntie Betty around, I kept myself safely tucked away.

What a shame it's your last day, Auntie Betty.

I've had a lovely time, Susan. I'll miss you all.

Mum, can we open the presents Auntie Betty left for us?

Yes, of course.

I wonder what they are.

A "sensible" jumper to cover my tummy button.

Auntie Betty will never change. She's left me a "How To Cook" book!

And what did Annie get? Pretty ribbons to keep her hair tidy . . .

. . . and a cat brush to get rid of my cat hairs!

The End

55

make it!

What you will need

loads of small safety pins all the same length

lots and lots of coloured mini beads – available in all good craft shops

scissors

elasticated thread

What to do

1 Open one of the safety pins and thread some of the beads on, then close the pin. You can use one colour or make a multi coloured pattern.

2 Do the same with all the other safety pins.

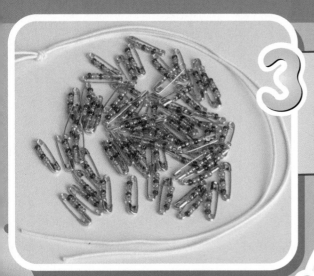

3 Cut 2 lengths of elastic thread, about 30cm each, and tie together loosely.

4 Thread the untied end of one of the threads through the top eyehole of a beaded safety pin. Now take the other untied end of thread and feed it through the bottom eyehole of the same pin.

5 String on the rest of the pins in the same way - make sure that you turn every second one upside down.

6 Carefully unknot the threads again and tie the ends together at the top and the bottom.

7 Snip any excess elastic off and your bracelet is ready to wear.

Wildlife

Wildlife
Dolphins

A dolphin can live from 25 to 65 years but, sadly, too few dolphins are reaching old age because they're being caught in

Just like you, dolphins enjoy chatting to their friends. Each dolphin can make about 30 different kinds of sound, including a personal whistle. Dolphins can also make clicks — up to 700 a second. Can you imagine a human chatterbox talking that fast?

fishing nets and drowning. Pollution is also killing dolphins. You can help them stay safe by doing beach clean ups and recycling your rubbish. Try to use less plastic as it's dangerous to dolphins.

Dolphins are mammals which means that they are warm-blooded, breathe air and feed their babies on milk.
Millions of years ago, dolphins lived on land, had body hair and front and hind limbs. Gradually they evolved to become more streamlined and flippers replaced their front limbs. A dolphin's tail is incredibly powerful with muscles six times stronger than the legs of a land mammal — maybe even a lion's.

Wildlife

Dolphin Diet

An average dolphin eats around 9 kilos of fish a day or up to one third of its own body weight, so a lot of fishing needs to be done. Dolphins go hunting together and often swim in line, side by side, looking for shoals of fish. When they find their tasty snack, a few dolphins circle the fish, making them rise to the surface. Next they make short bursts of clicks at the fish so that they scatter and the dolphins pick out individual fish. If a fish nearly gets away, the dolphin will use his tail to bat it into the air to stun it.

Clickety-click

It's not always easy to see underwater so dolphins need more than eyesight to get around and find food at night. They have an amazing way of finding out what's going on in their watery world. It's called echo location and it works by the dolphins producing "clicks". These are sent out like a torch beam from their bulging foreheads and the echoes that bounce back from objects in the water make vibrations. The dolphins then feel the vibrations in the teeth of their lower jaws. These "moving sound messages" travel along to the dolphins' ears next. Using echo location, a bottlenose dolphin can pinpoint an object the size of a small orange over 100 metres away! Amazing!

Dolphins have around 164 sharp teeth with which to grab their food and, because they are mammals, they have more than one type of tooth — just like us. Their ears are seen only as a tiny hole a few centimetres behind each eye but dolphins have inner ears and can hear very well.

Some dolphins' clicking sounds are so high, our ears can't even hear them. It's said that the only living thing that can make a higher-pitched sound than Mariah Carey is a dolphin.

The shape of their mouths makes dolphins look as if they're smiling. It's hard to believe that they're actually related to killer whales!

Playtime

Dolphins love to play by rolling, spinning and leaping alongside each other.

Playing and feeding together are important bonding times for groups of dolphins. They hate to be alone and wild dolphins have often been seen swimming and playing with people!

One of their games is called bow-riding when they swim along next to ships, jump out of the water and do somersaults! Some people believe dolphins are playing and squealing with delight when they ride a ship's bow waves in the sea. Others think the dolphins are just hitching a ride to save their energy. Only the dolphins know the answer to that but it certainly sounds fun!

It has been noticed that dolphins that live in dolphinariums or marinas make up their own games. Some lie on the bottom of the pool and blow bubbles to hear the different sounds they make while others like to carry a small turtle on their noses to give it a ride around the pool! Playing helps to develop the dolphins' muscles and skills.

Dolphins

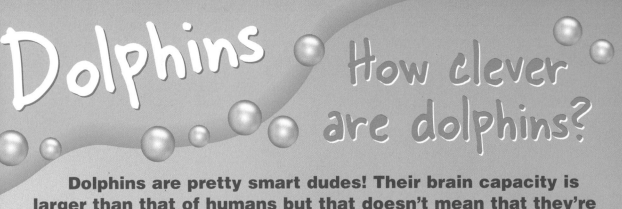

How clever are dolphins?

Dolphins are pretty smart dudes! Their brain capacity is larger than that of humans but that doesn't mean that they're more intelligent. They can, however, remember a sequence of notes half an hour long and repeat the sequence exactly. Wow! Imagine being able to repeat every word your teacher said in a lesson!

Naughty

Dolphins hate being told "no!" and can sometimes be naughty. One story goes that a few dolphins were being trained in Hawaii. When they touched the Frisbee, they were given a "yes" signal and also a treat as a reward. If they went wrong, though, they were told "no!" and got no treat. They didn't like the "no!" signal and especially no treat so the dolphins picked up the Frisbees and aimed them at their trainer. The trainer soon stopped saying "no!" and turned her back on the dolphins instead. This worked well and, after a few months, the dolphins scored 85% in their exams. Maybe they should sit yours for you at school?

Wildlife

Wildlife
Dolphins

Helping People

Special therapy programmes exist where a swim with a live dolphin is offered to help children with speech problems. When the dolphins make their clicks in the water, the sounds can reprogramme a human brain — a bit like adding a new programme to your computer!

In some cases, dolphins can also help poorly people feel better. Their smiley faces can relax and make them feel happy.

Dolphins have saved many people from drowning. Just in the same way as they push their babies to the surface to breathe when they're born, they instinctively push people who are having difficulty in the water to the surface for air.

Scientists believe that when we're really happy, our brains produce special painkillers called endorphins and sometimes interferon, a protein which can boost the immune system. The dolphins love to play and have their tummies stroked, making a relaxing atmosphere all round.

For some very poorly children, the Make-A-Wish Foundation offers them the chance to swim with dolphins and put a smile on their faces. If you'd like to find out more, write to: Make-A-Wish Foundation UK, 329-331 London Road, Camberley, Surrey, GU15 3HQ.

Wildlife

dolph puzz

WILD WORDSEARCH

Clifford's diving into this wild wordsearch to find the different types of dolphin listed below. The words can read backwards, forwards, up, down or diagonally.

BOTTLENOSE
CHINESE RIVER
HOURGLASS
HUMPBACK
ORCA
PORPOISE
RISSO'S
SPINNER
SPOTTED
STRIPED
WHALE
WHITE BEAKED

The word POD appears at least 24 times. How many times can *you* find it?

HOW MANY

How many words of three letters or more can you make from

ECHO LOCATION?

1-12 good **13-18 fintastic**
19 and over flip-tastic!

D	E	S	O	N	E	L	T	T	O	B	D
E	E	D	R	A	E	D	O	P	D	O	P
T	O	K	C	L	P	O	D	O	P	D	R
T	S	S	A	L	G	R	U	O	H	D	E
O	P	H	D	E	L	A	R	H	P	O	N
P	W	K	C	A	B	P	M	U	H	P	N
S	H	D	O	P	O	E	O	L	O	O	I
O	P	S	P	I	P	N	T	D	X	D	P
S	O	O	S	O	D	E	P	I	R	T	S
S	D	E	D	O	P	O	D	O	H	A	W
I	D	O	P	O	D	O	P	O	D	W	L
R	E	V	I	R	E	S	E	N	I	H	C

FISHY FOOD

Help Candie unscramble these letters to find Dolly Dolphin's fave fishy foods.

NAUT

DUISQ

ULMELT

68

CATCH YOUR TAIL

Put the answers to the clues in the grid. The *last* letter of each word is the *first* letter of the next.

1. A baby dolphin is called a _ _ _ _.
2. A dolphin's "arm".
3. A turn in the water.
4. A jump in the air.
5. A small kind of dolphin.
6. This helps a dolphin see and hear. We've helped you with this one.

1.

6.   2.

5.   T   I

A   O

N

C

O   L

4.

3.

FUN TIME

Score out the letters that appear 3 times in each word square and the remaining ones will spell out fun things for dolphins to do.

Ⓐ
R	N	L	D
E	R	O	N
A	D	O	D
N	O	R	P

Ⓑ
S	T	E	P
X	A	X	E
A	I	T	A
N	E	X	T

Ⓒ
M	D	O	S
I	V	T	S
T	M	T	O
M	S	O	E

Ⓓ
S	W	U	R
U	S	I	W
O	I	U	I
L	S	W	L

SPOT THE DIFFERENCES

Can you find six differences between these two pictures of Poppy and Suzi playing with a dolphin?

ANSWERS

FISHY FOOD: **Tuna, Squid, Mullet.** CATCH YOUR TAIL: 1.Calf, 2.Flipper, 3.Roll, 4.Leap, 5.Porpoise, 6.Echo location. FUN TIME: a.leap, b.spin, c.dive, d.roll.

the perfect

Do you dream of having a pet? Well, small pets make fantastic pets, so try our quiz and find out which mini pet is the one for you.

Do you have a lot of spare time?

n — **Would you mind clearing up after your pet?**

Y — **Do you want to be a vet when you grow up?**

Is Animals and You your favourite magazine?

h

Y

n

h

n — **Have you ever looked after a pet before?**

Y

Would you be allowed to keep 2 animals?

Y

n

Is anyone in your house allergic to fur?

n

h

Y

Have you got room for a huge cage?

Y

n

Are you a patient person?

Y

goldfish

budgie

guinea pig, hamster

pet

goldfish

A goldfish would be the perfect pet for you. You're a busy person and wouldn't have time to clean out a pet's cage every day. Also, if you haven't had a pet before, a fish is a great first time pet. You could maybe think about getting a bigger pet when you have more time to spend with it.

budgie

Budgies need quite a big cage so they have plenty of room to flap about. Their cage will need cleaned out at least once a week and will need fresh water and seed every day. If you spend a lot of time with your budgie then it will become quite tame and may even learn to speak!

guinea pig, hamster

A small pet like a guinea pig, hamster or gerbil would be great for you. They need a nice big cage or hutch to live in and lots of interesting toys to play with. You'll need to be prepared to change their bedding every day and give them fresh water and food in their food bowls. You also have to remember that hamsters sleep during the day and are active at night so you'll need to be patient if you want to play with them.

Turn the page to find out some fascinating facts about your furry, fishy or feathered little friend.

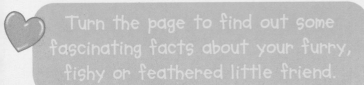

budgie

Budgies live in the wild in Australia.

Their official name is budgerigar, budgie for short.

The word budgerigar comes from the native Australian word 'betcherrygah' which means 'good to eat'!

The natural colour for a budgie in the wild is light green.

The budgie is the most popular pet bird in the world.

Male budgies have a blue bit above their beak and the female's is brown.

hamster

Hamsters will hibernate when the temperature drops below 5°C (41°F).

Wild hamsters live in hot areas of Central Asia.

The name hamster comes from the German word 'hamstern' which means 'to hoard'.

Hamsters can store up to half their body weight in their cheek pouches!

Baby hamsters are called pups.

They can travel up to 8 miles a night in search of food.

Guinea pigs are also called Cavy.

They are not related to pigs!

guinea pig

Guinea pigs come from South America where they still live in the wild.

When they are happy, guinea pigs will purr!

Babies are born with all their fur and their eyes open.

A male guinea pig is called a boar, a female is a sow.

There are about 20 different species of guinea pig.

Babies are called piglets – aww!

Goldfish are actually very intelligent and will recognise the person who feeds them.

goldfish

There are over 300 kinds of goldfish.

They eat both plants and little water animals.

The oldest known goldfish lived to be 43 years old!

Goldfish lay eggs which attach to underwater plants.

A female can produce thousands and thousands of eggs.

These eggs will hatch in under a week.

girls r great!

It's all about you and your friends!

bestest buds

Be the best pal a girl could ever have. Your mate's sure to smile if you -

* give her a friendship bracelet – every time she looks at it she'll know you're always there for her

* tell her she looks gorgeous – just like Cat Deeley

* make her a tape of all the songs the two of you love to listen to

* lend her your most fave necklace to finish off her party outfit to perfection

* let her go on and on about all her probs and not yawn once

* send her a text telling her how fab she is

smile!
Add some funky little animal smileys to the texts and emails you send to your friends -

dog (:o-<)

cat >o0~

duck {:\/

koala @(*o*)@

fish <><

big fish >-^(;>

frog 8)

pig :8)

mouse <:3()~~~

monkey := l

friend check

Answer these fun questions to find out how much you know about your pal - then get her to answer them about you. Score one point for each correct answer.

* Which of these does she like best?
cinema
disco
sleepover party

* Her dream holiday is?
hot tropical beach
theme park
activity centre

* Which pop star or band does she go totally mad for?

* What's her fave outfit?
Funky jeans and a cute t-shirt
Loose and baggy skater style
Girly and glittery top and skirt

* Name your best mate's fave
colour
video or film
tv show
shop
food

Get your mate rate -

1 - 3: Are you sure you're pals? You hardly know your friend! Spend less time talking about yourself and find out more about your mate.

4 - 6: The two of you are pretty good pals, but you're not **best** best friends. Maybe you only see each other at school.

7 - 9: You are great mates. You know lots of stuff about your pal. Well done.

2gether

Cool things to do with your best bud -

* watch a video and share the biggest bar of choccy you can find

* go to the photo booth and get some piccies taken together

* give each other a glitter-tastic disco makeover

* read every fab issue of Animals and You monthly

* share and swap clothes – two wardrobes have gotta be better than one!

* Turn the page to try out our cool Friendship Finder

friendship finder

Wanna find out what kind of mate your best bud really is? It's easy with our funky Friendship Finder. Here's what to do ...

Count out how many letters are in your friend's first name and last name and add the two numbers together. For example -

LOUISE GIBSON
6 + 6 = 12

• If the answer is 10 or more, add the digits of the answer together to get a single number -

1 + 2 = 3

• That gives you a friendship score of 3, so go to the wheel and beginning at the START section, count round 3 boxes in a CLOCKWISE direction. Whichever animal you end up on will reveal all about your mate.

puppy
Your friend is bursting with energy and always on the go. She loves any kind of party, disco or sleepover and is always laughing. If you're feeling sad she'll cheer you up in 5 minutes flat. You'll never be bored around this girl.

kitten
She's a cool fashion friend. Saturdays are for shopping, sweetie! She knows what all the latest styles and looks are and tries them all. Want a make-over or funky new hair do? She's the one to ask. You'll look kitty-licious in no time at all. Fab!

guinea pig
This girl is a bit on the quiet and shy side. It takes ages to get to know her, but once you do, she makes a great mate. She'll listen to all your problems, stick up for you and always be there when you need her. And when she gets over her shyness, she's brilliant fun too.

rabbit
Oops! She sometimes speaks before she thinks and can appear rude, but she's really a good pal. She doesn't mean to offend and would never be nasty on purpose. She's funny and comes up with all the best jokes and schemes.

elephant
She's always got a plan for something to do and somewhere to go and doesn't mind who tags along. She's happy for anyone to join in the fun and is very easy-going. But watch out if you cross her. This mate won't forget and finds it very hard to forgive.

panda
She's a bestest bud girl. You get on really well together and can't imagine ever falling out. Sometimes you know what she's going to say or you might even finish each other's sentences. You can trust her with your biggest secrets - she won't ever blab.

START

tiger
puppy
kitten
lion
guinea pig
parrot
panda
elephant
rabbit

parrot ⭐

She's super-friendly and makes mates wherever she goes. You'll meet lots of new people when you're with her. She's easy to get on with and likes a laugh. This girl knows all the latest goss and is a gold medal chatterbox - you won't be able to shut her up!

lion

Wow! This girl likes to take the lead. She can organise for Britain and won't take no for an answer. You won't get a chance to relax around her cos she just doesn't do lazy. She has a quick temper, but she's never angry for long. The good thing is, plans never go wrong when she's in charge.

tiger

She seems lovely and friendly and usually is. But sometimes she can be a bit selfish. If she wants something, expect a huge strop until she gets her own way. The same goes for her time - she might not be in the mood to deal with your probs, but you'll always have to listen to hers.

Continued from page 39

The riders were caught in a storm —

Wendy

Everyone keep close together as we cross this stream.

At the other side —

Are you all okay?

Just a bit wet.

But then —

Aah! Lightning!

Take it easy, Ellen. You'll spook Apache.

Unsettled, Apache suddenly bolted.

Stay there, everyone. Wendy, take charge!

Mark galloped after Apache.

Stop, Apache, stop!

Mark's headed him off — thank goodness!

Easy, boy! You're all right now.

Oh, thanks, Mark. That was scary.

I've fixed a leading rein to Apache so he can't do that again.

Some of the other ponies are getting restless too.

We'll have to abandon our plans to go straight back to Rose Lodge. Let's see if we can find shelter until the storm has passed.

Meanwhile at Rose Lodge —

Any sign of the riders, Mr Thornley?

No, John. Mark expected to be back just after six.

It's nearly quarter to seven. I wouldn't normally worry, but in this weather . . . I'm contacting the police.

79

Wendy's best friend, Bianca, was police inspector Kramer's daughter.

That was Mr Thornley. Wendy and Mark haven't come back from their picnic with some riders. He's worried.

Oh, no! I hope they're okay.

I'm going over to Rose Lodge.

Let me know if you hear anything, Dad.

Meanwhile, the riders found a cottage.

Let's see if there's anyone home.

There's nobody here and the door's unlocked.

It's usually rented out as a holiday cottage.

I don't think anyone will mind if we take shelter. But first we'll get the horses into the barn.

Right, everyone. Lead your ponies and follow me.

next —

I wonder what food we have left . . . oh, Patrick!

Oops!

I tripped over this wire.

It's a phone wire. Let's try the phone.

I'll phone Dad and tell him where we are.

Dad? It's Wendy.

What's happened? Is everything all right?

Well, we had a bit of a problem with Ellen and . . .

Just then, lightning struck the telegraph pole outside.

Wendy! Wendy! I can't hear you.

The line's gone dead.

Did she say where they were?

No, only that they'd had a problem with Ellen.

What's that about my daughter?

The children's parents had turned up.

Where are our children, Mr Thornley?

I'm afraid they're not back yet.

But you know where they are?

No, I don't. Wendy was cut off before she could tell me.

Please don't worry. Wherever they are, they have shelter. And Wendy and Mark are very sensible.

Wendy's just a child!

82

You're not fit to run stables, letting a young girl take charge!

Calm down, sir. I'm sure they're safe wherever they are.

Continued on page 104

cute!

Do you know what a puggle is? Ever heard of ephyna? Find out what they are right here ...

We're all used to puppy dogs, but other creatures that have babies called pups include armadillos, bats, moles, otters, squirrels and sharks.

Another name for a lamb is a cosset.

Little hares are called leverets and baby rabbits are kittens.

Puggles are babies belonging to the duck-billed platypus and echidnas (spiny anteaters).

Wriggly baby eels are known as elvers.

An ephyna is a baby jellyfish! Baby fish are called fry.

Kangaroos, koala bears, wallabies, wombats and opossums have babies called joeys.

Think you've never seen a polliwog? Chances are you have – it's another name for tadpole.

Not all baby birds are chicks. Little owls are owlets, hawks are eyas, pigeons and doves are squabs, turkeys are poults and swans are cygnets.

Lots of animals have babies known as calves. These include antelopes, moose, camels, dolphins and whales, elephants, giraffes and hippos.

A cria is a llama baby.

chat about cats!

Hi, Cat Cool Girl here with lots of kitty-licious info. Did you know ...?

* Cats can't taste sweet things. They only have taste buds along the edges and at the back of their tongues. The rough bit in the middle is specially for cleaning their fur.

● Kittens have 26 very sharp milk teeth. These are replaced by 30 adult teeth by the time they are 6 months old.

● Only tiny kittens need cat milk. After they're 3 weeks old it's better to give them water. Ordinary cow's milk can upset your cat's tummy.

* Cats can see especially well at dusk and dawn – the best hunting times – and have excellent hearing.

* Lots of cats hate collars. It's best to get your kitten microchipped in case it gets lost. Chipping only takes a minute and doesn't hurt. Ask your vet for more info.

● They can smell through their mouths as well as their noses! A special bit in the roof of a cat's mouth lets them do this.

* Cats don't like vinegar or citrus smells. If your kitten has any little accidents, rub in some vinegar or citronella oil after you've cleaned up the mess.

● Kittens love to play but need lots of sleep too. If your kitten is resting it's best to leave it in peace.

● Cat poo can kill plants, so sprinkle lemon or orange peel round the garden. This should stop them from doing the loo next to Mum and Dad's prize flowers.

* Clever kitties don't take long to house train. Encourage a kitten to use a litter tray by sitting it in the tray and gently grazing one of its paws over the litter.

kitty search

Get your paws on a pen and try to find all these breeds of cats in this purr-fect puzzle! The words can be found reading up, down, backwards, forwards and diagonally.

ABYSSINIAN
ANGORA
BALINESE
BENGAL
BIRMAN
BURMESE
CHARTREUX
DEVON REX

HIMALAYAN
JAVANESE
KORAT
MAINE COON
MANX
NEBELUNG
NORWEGIAN FOREST
OCICAT

ORIENTAL
PERSIAN
RAGDOLL
RUSSIAN BLUE
SIAMESE
SNOWSHOE
SPHYNX
TURKISH VAN

B	A	L	I	N	E	S	E	K	R	U	T	J	A	N	R	O
N	I	A	B	O	O	C	E	N	A	M	U	A	E	O	A	R
O	C	R	X	U	E	R	T	R	A	A	R	V	S	O	G	I
R	H	I	M	A	L	A	Y	A	N	I	K	A	E	I	B	E
W	A	X	O	A	B	Y	S	S	I	N	I	A	N	S	U	N
E	R	A	N	M	N	M	I	P	O	E	H	N	A	R	R	T
G	T	B	E	Y	A	A	A	E	N	C	S	S	V	E	M	A
I	R	Y	B	T	H	N	M	R	R	O	G	N	A	P	E	L
A	E	S	E	U	E	P	E	S	M	O	L	B	J	H	S	A
N	U	S	L	R	U	S	S	I	A	N	B	L	U	E	E	G
F	X	Y	U	K	A	A	E	A	B	M	A	U	B	O	T	N
O	B	S	N	I	N	G	N	N	O	N	E	S	C	H	U	E
R	E	I	G	S	E	A	D	G	G	X	P	I	M	S	R	B
E	N	N	E	H	S	I	A	O	O	H	C	M	A	W	O	I
S	G	O	I	V	N	S	R	C	L	A	T	A	R	O	K	R
T	A	N	R	A	M	A	N	O	T	L	A	L	X	N	A	M
D	E	V	O	N	R	E	X	C	N	X	Y	H	P	S	M	A

85

© PhotoDisc

cool hairstyles

Funky Bunches

1 Put your hair in bunches using coloured elastic hair bands.

2 Now get more coloured bands and put them in the whole way down both bunches. Leave about 4 or 5 cm between each band.

3 Now tease apart the section of hair between the bands.

4 The finished look!

This is a great hairstyle for school. It keeps your hair tidy and away from your face, but also looks funky too!

86

Lotsa' Knots

1 Divide your hair into little sections all over your head. Take one section and pin the rest out of the way.

2 Twist this section really tightly until it starts to turn in on itself.

3 Now twist it up into a mini bun and pin it with some grips.

4 Do the same with the rest of the sections. Try to make them as tight as possible.

5 Take some coloured bands and tie them round the buns for the finished look.

This look takes a bit of time and patience, but it's a cool style for a party or disco. When you take your hair down afterwards, you'll be left with luscious curls as well – two hairstyles from one!

What you will need

make

A pair of old jeans

scissors

needle and thread

ribbon or anything suitable as a strap

pieces of material

fabric paint, patches, sequins, beads or anything to decorate the bag with

MAKE SURE THE JEANS ARE OLD AND YOU ARE ALLOWED TO CUT THEM UP!

What to do

1

Ask an adult to help you cut off the back pocket of an old pair of jeans. Be careful to cut outside the seam so the pocket stays in one piece.

Sew a long piece of ribbon, or whatever you are using as a strap, to the sides of the pockets. You can decide how long it should be by measuring it against yourself.

2

¡it!

3 Next, decorate the outside of the pocket using whatever you like. You can use fabric paints to paint a design, sew beads on, or simply stick on some old bits of material.

4 Stick or sew your decorations on your bag.

5 You can make a different style of bag out of the other pocket.

Snoop's STORY

Regular readers of Animals and **R**You monthly know that Snoop's our doggy friend of the stars. He gives us all the latest goss on celebs.

Not so many people know about Snoop's sad start in life, though.

When he was only 8 weeks old, Snoop was tied up in a carrier bag and left lying in town beside some rubbish. Luckily, a passer-by spotted the bag moving and took Snoop along to the local animal shelter. It was the week after Christmas and Snoop joined other pups who'd been abandoned too — probably all unwanted Christmas presents.

Homes had to be found urgently for all the pups so Snoop's photo and story were printed in the local newspaper. Lots of people fell in love with the pup and offered him a loving home but the conditions had to be right. A new puppy needs lots of time and care. Eventually, a family was chosen to care for Snoop.

in a carrier bag and left for dead in

c -t a i deades srgssgl errioed"

months, and it would be   home should contact Mrs

The little pup had a garden to run around and grow up in and was so happy with his new family.

The following Christmas was completely different for Snoop. Instead of being cruelly dumped all alone in a carrier bag, he was surrounded by people who loved him. He even had his own stack of Christmas presents — including his favourite squeaky cracker which drove everyone mad!

Snoop is still with his family and comes into the Animals and You office every month to give us his news.

Turn the page to find some famous faces . . .

What do all these famous faces have in common? They all won telly talent shows!

Popstars

This was the first show and the winner was a band called Hear'Say with a hit called Pure and Simple. Kym Marsh has since left the band and become a solo singer.

Pop Idol

Lots of lovely lads had success following that show. Will Young was the winner with Evergreen but Gareth Gates and Darius Danesh didn't miss out! They both have a string of hits to their names.

Pop Stars: The Rivals

This was the battle of the bands — girls versus boys! The girl band, Girls Aloud, beat the boys, One True Voice, with their single, Sounds of the Underground.

Fame Academy

David Sneddon won this fab TV talent contest with a song he wrote himself, Living the Lie. Fame Academy's runner-up, Sinead Quinn, also had a huge hit with I Can't Break Down.

So, if you think you've got talent, don't be too shy to enter a talent competition!

BUNNY

ABC

As sweet as can be — that's a
bunny! Read on to find out more
about these perfect pets.

ADORABLE

Rabbits are so cute no wonder they're almost taking over from cats as our favourite pet. But although they look like fluffy toys, you have to think carefully before keeping one as a pet. A healthy rabbit can live for 6 - 8 years and it needs a caring and loving owner to look after it.

BREEDS

There are lots of different breeds, but some like the Flemish Giant can grow to be as big as a dog! So smaller breeds like the Rex, Dwarf and Lop make the best pets. Dwarf Lops with their floppy ears are very popular bunnies as they are usually friendly and good natured.

CARING

Short haired rabbits don't need much grooming, but the fluffy Angora rabbits must have their long hair brushed every day. When carrying your bunny always pick it up by its body (never the ears) and support its hind legs with your hand.

Rabbits can live indoors or outdoors. If your bunny lives outside, its hutch must be cleaned once every week and dirty bedding removed every day.

Homes where bunnies are kept indoors have to be bunny-proofed! This means making sure there are no dangerous wires around for them to chew. House rabbits can even be litter trained.

DID YOU KNOW?

A female rabbit is called a doe.

A male rabbit is called a buck.

A baby rabbit is called a kitten.

Lettuce leaves are not good for bunnies.

Pink-eyed rabbits have poor eyesight.

Lop-eared rabbits can't hear very well.

Animals and You readers' top bunny name is Fluffy.

If your bunny is in the huff, he will turn his back on you!

Wildlife

Wildlife

Lions

Lions mainly live in Africa, although the Asiatic lion lives in north west India. They live in grasslands where they can hide in the long grass.

Cute Cubs

- Cubs are born with spotted coats. This disappears as they grow older.

- They are born in litters of about 2 - 6 cubs.

- Male cubs will start growing their mane at the age of 18 months.

- All the females in the group will help to look after the cubs.

Family Pride

Lions live in big groups called prides. Each pride can contain anything from 4 to 40 lions. The pride usually consists of a big group of females who are all related, their cubs and 1 to 5 adult males who defend the pride.

Feline Facts

- You can hear a lion's roar up to 5 miles away.

- Lions spend about 20 hours of the day dozing.

- They are the largest of the African big cats.

- Lions are the only big cats to live in big family groups.

- Lions will rub cheeks to greet each other.

- The Swahili word for lion is Simba - just like the Lion King!

Wildlife

Tigers

There are 5 different kinds of tiger which live in different countries in the world.

Siberian

● Siberian tigers are the largest of all the tiger species with males growing up to 3.3 metres long (10 feet 9 inches).

● Siberian tigers are quite a pale orange colour and they have less stripes than the other tigers.

● They also have a white tummy and thick ruff round their neck to keep them cosy as they live in the cold.

Bengal

● These tigers can live in the freezing cold temperatures of high mountains or in the hot and steamy swamps and hills of India.

● White Bengal tigers exist in the wild.

● They basically have white fur and dark brown or reddish stripes. However, they are very rare.

Indo Chinese

● The Indo Chinese tiger is smaller than the Bengal tiger and has a darker orange fur.

● Their stripes are shorter and quite narrow.

● They live in remote forests or mountains in south east Asia.

South China Tiger

- These tigers are one of the most endangered in the world.

- At the moment, there is thought to be as few as 20 - 30 still in the wild.

- They live in southern China.

Stripy Cubs

Mum brings up the babies on her own. She will normally give birth to 2 or 3 cubs. When they are born, cubs are blind and very weak. Even from birth tigers have their stripy pattern. They only weigh 1 kg (2 to 3 pounds) at birth. For the first 6 - 8 weeks of their lives they will live on Mum's milk and then they will follow her on hunts.

Sumatran

- These tigers are only found on the island of Sumatra, near India.

- The Sumatran tiger is also the smallest species of tiger and grows to be about 2.4 metres (8 feet).

- They have the darkest orange fur of all the tigers and have very broad stripes which are very close together.

Tiger Tips

- Tigers can see in colour.

- They can see 6 times better than humans.

- A group of tigers is called a streak.

- Paw prints are called pug marks.

- No two tigers have the same pattern of stripes.

101

Wildlife

Leopards

There are 20 different species of leopard which include the snow leopard and the clouded leopard. They can be found living in South Africa, India, China and Siberia.

Lovely Leopards

- Leopards have pale yellow fur and are covered in dark rosette markings.

- A fully grown leopard can measure up to $1\frac{1}{2}$ metres (5 feet) long and their tails can be another 90cm (3 feet).

- They can live up to 15 years.

- No two leopards have the same pattern of rosettes.

Leopard Lunch

- Leopards will eat anything from dung beetles (yuk!) to young giraffe.

- Leopards do most of their hunting at night.

- They are so powerful that they can carry a huge animal into the trees so no other animal pinches it!

- They can survive for quite a long time without water.

- They follow their prey quietly and then jump out on them when they least expect it.

Cuddly Cubs

- Leopard cubs are born with spots but have darker fur.

- They only weigh 1 or 2 pounds (1kg) at birth and are blind and have no fur.

- By 3 months old they are ready to follow Mum on hunts.

- Cubs follow the tuft on Mum's tail so they don't get lost.

Wildlife

continued from page 82

The riders had shelter in an empty cottage —

How are the horses, Mark?

They're fine in this barn.

Wendy

Now the horses are settled, we'll get a fire going in the cottage.

Here's some wood.

Wendy calmed her horse, Penny.

Don't worry, girl. We'll soon be back home.

Indoors —

We've got the fire going.

I'm hungry. Can we have something to eat?

Good idea!

There's not a lot of food. We'll have to keep some for morning.

Meanwhile, at Rose Lodge —

Any news yet?

No, Mrs Thornley — nothing.

Don't worry, Helen. They're sensible. They'll be okay.

I hope Mum's right.

The storm was still raging.

More lightning! I'm scared!

I'll have to take her mind off the storm. She'll scare the others.

Right, now we've eaten, let's hold a fashion show.

What do you mean? There aren't any clothes here.

We can dress up, starting with this rug . . .

. . . and now you see Wendy Thornley wearing the latest wrapover skirt!

You're so cool, Wendy!

And later —

Let's tell each other funny stories! I remember once . . .

Well done, Wendy. They've forgotten about the storm now.

But the horses are upset again. I can hear them whinnying. I'll go and see to them.

Steady, Benny. Calm down, all of you.

Soon —

Now that they're settled again, I'll get some rest too.

106

At home, plans were being made —

I'll pack some food for you to take.

Good idea. They're bound to be hungry. We'll leave at first light.

Oh, Charles! The children will be all right, won't they?

Of course! Mark and Wendy will take care of them.

Early next morning —

My daughter had better be all right.

I'm sure she will. Wait here.

I'll call on my mobile when I have news.

We'll take the picnic ride trail, Mr Thornley.

Thanks, John.

Good luck. I'll call you if we see anything.

Same here.

At the cottage —

Wake up, everybody! The storm's over. It's a lovely day.

We'd better get back to Rose Lodge as soon as possible in case the weather breaks again.

As they saddled up —

Follow carefully because the ground is very slippery.

After a short time —

Look! There's Dad!

Back at Rose Lodge —

Thank goodness you're safe. Is anyone hurt?

No. We're all fine, Dad.

I'm glad my daughter's safe, but you haven't heard the last of this, Thornley!

But, Dad, Mark saved me when my pony bolted and Wendy kept us happy last night. They were great!

Yeah! We had great fun in the cottage.

It's the best picnic ride I've ever been on!

108

It seems I have an apology to make.

It's okay. You were just worried — like any good parent.

I'm proud of you, Wendy. Well done!

Thanks, Dad!

THE END

CARING FOR A PONY

If you'd like to have your own pony, then be prepared for lots of hard work. Morven and Mhairi Miller have been riding for years and here's how they look after their six ponies.

Every day, the girls greet their ponies with a cuddle then put fresh water in their stalls and prepare their feeds. Next they hang up their haynets — and that's before they set off for school!

Later, the stalls have to be mucked out — yuk! — the ponies groomed and then, the fun bit —

exercised! The girls and their ponies love riding together and compete in horse shows all over Britain. All their hard work's well worth it when they win rosettes and trophies.

111

Later —

Well, I have.

Tell me, Mum!

You know old Mrs Wilkins who lives at number four?

Yes.

I said you'd do her weekly shopping in return for a small donation.

Next day —

And she said that one of her friends might want her shopping done too!

Brilliant! I could definitely do that!

This is going to be such a help, Daisy.

And you'll be helping me to help those poor rescue donkeys.

Here's my shopping list and here's Mrs Simon's.

Right, see you soon.

But —

Easy peasy, Digger, and each trip I do will earn £ for the sanctuary.

Oh, dear — I'm in such a muddle and losing the shopping lists didn't help!

Phew, this is harder than I thought — and stop getting under my feet, Digger!

Next day —

Will Daisy raise the money?
Turn to page 120...

LET'S SHOP

Lots of shopping puzzles to keep you busy for ages!

pet store

Unscramble the letters to reveal 5 animals and fit them into the grid.
Unscramble the letters in the shaded squares to find the cute creatures Candie saw at the pet shop.

SARTMEH
GEBLIR
SEUMO
GUANIE PGI
TINKET

bags of bags

Suzi has dropped one of her bags on the way home from the shops. Lead her back through this mega maze to find it.

poppy parties

Poppy is planning a huuuge party. Fill in the missing letters to find out what goodies she has in her shopping basket.

__ __ L _ O _ _ S

_ E M _ _ A _ _

S T _ _ _ M _ R _

_ C _ C _ _ A M

_ _ K E _

P _ _ Z _

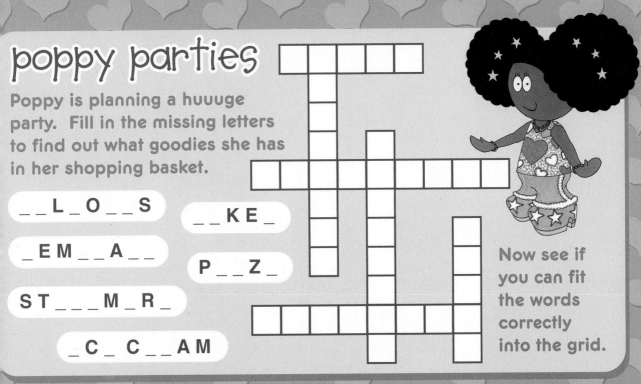

Now see if you can fit the words correctly into the grid.

Boing!

Look what Cat got at the shopping mall - a super-springy space hopper! See how many words of 3 or more letters you can make from

shopping mall

10 – 15: good!
16 – 25: **great!**
more than 25: groovy!

answers

fashion-tastic!

Fi-Fi has bought a fabulous new outfit. Fill in the empty squares with a number between 1 and 5 so that all the rows, columns and diagonals add up correctly. Now add all the missing numbers together to find out how much she's spent.

Hint: add up the lines with one missing number first to start you off.

						25
2	4			3	3	18
2		4	3	5	4	21
		1	2		2	18
3	1	3	2	4		17
3		1	3	4	5	21
4	5	1	1	3	4	18
19	19	12	19	21	23	17

rescued!

When Charlie, the black Labrador cross, left Battersea Dogs Home to start a new life, nobody knew just how exciting and exotic it would be.

Charlie was originally chosen by the Canine Unit of the Royal Army Veterinary Corps (RAVC) to train as an expert in sniffing out drugs, explosives and people. Then the RAVC received a request from the Kenyan Wildlife Service for help and Charlie was picked as one of the first ever dogs to be trained to find ivory.

Sadly, even though trading in ivory has been banned worldwide, elephants and rhino are still killed by poachers who want their tusks and horns. In Kenya some poachers bury the tusks for years and go back for them when people are no longer looking for them. It would be Charlie's job to sniff out these hoards.

Special permission was given for some ivory to be brought to England for the training programme. Every time the dogs found the hidden ivory they were rewarded and a huge fuss was made of them. They soon began to associate the smell of ivory with fun and praise. As a result, they love their job, as well as being very good at it!

After 12 weeks it was time for Charlie and his friends to move to Lake Naivasha in Kenya. Working in the hot Kenyan savanna is very different from life in Britain, so special kennels had to be designed and built by army engineers to make sure all the dogs would be comfortable and happy.

In Kenya, dogs are not regarded as family pets, so the new local handlers had to be trained too! They were taught the loving care and reward system that the dogs were used to. Grooming, walking and giving the dogs plenty of attention were all part of the course. Charlie and his handler, Robert, who is a Masai Ranger, are now best friends.

The dogs quickly became used to the sights, smells and sounds of their new home and are doing a fantastic job helping combat poaching in Kenya. And after a hard day's work, Charlie loves to relax with a walk past the giraffes and splash in the lake.

Charlie has gone from being a rescue dog at Battersea to helping rescue other animals. Well done, Charlie!

all about Battersea Dogs Home

Battersea Dogs Home

In 1860 Mrs Mary Tealby opened The Temporary Home for Lost and Starving Dogs in a stable yard in Holloway, London. It moved to the Battersea site in 1871 and in 1885 was renamed The Dogs' Home Battersea. Today there are 3 centres at Battersea, Brands Hatch and Old Windsor caring for over 9700 dogs and 2700 cats a year. Phew!

Dogs and cats stay at Battersea until they are reunited with their owners or for as long as it takes to find the perfect new home for them.

All animals are checked over by a team of veterinary nurses, vaccinated and microchipped before leaving the Home, and many are neutered. It costs £70 to rehome a Battersea dog and £40 for a cat.

For more info on all the Battersea services, rehoming, fundraising ideas and fun things to do log on to

www.dogshome.org

Remember to ask an adult first.

122

123

Oh, dear, Digger. I do feel bad.

And you were supposed to be helping – not hindering, Digger!

It was really good of Mr Peters to give me £4 for the donkey sanctuary.

But I've still got a long way to go before I reach my target!

I wonder if anyone wants any decorating done? It looks dead easy on the TV.